T0318499

Cambridge Elements ≡

Elements in Modern Wars

THE CULTURAL HISTORY OF WAR IN THE TWENTIETH CENTURY AND AFTER

Jay Winter
Yale University

Shaftesbury Road, Cambridge CB2 8EA, United Kingdom

One Liberty Plaza, 20th Floor, New York, NY 10006, USA

477 Williamstown Road, Port Melbourne, VIC 3207, Australia

314–321, 3rd Floor, Plot 3, Splendor Forum, Jasola District Centre,
New Delhi – 110025, India

103 Penang Road, #05–06/07, Visioncrest Commercial, Singapore 238467

Cambridge University Press is part of Cambridge University Press & Assessment,
a department of the University of Cambridge.

We share the University's mission to contribute to society through the pursuit of
education, learning and research at the highest international levels of excellence.

www.cambridge.org
Information on this title: www.cambridge.org/9781009114271
DOI: 10.1017/9781009110303

First published 2022

A catalogue record for this publication is available from the British Library.

ISBN 978-1-009-11427-1 Paperback
ISSN 2633-8378 (online)
ISSN 2633-836X (print)

The Cultural History of War in the Twentieth Century and After

Elements in Modern Wars

DOI: 10.1017/9781009110303
First published online: August 2022

Jay Winter
Yale University
Author for correspondence: Jay Winter, jay.winter@yale.edu

Abstract: This Element is a user's guide to the cultural history of warfare since 1914. It provides summaries of the basic questions historians have posed in what is now a truly global field of research. It is divided into three parts. The first part provides an introduction to the cultural history of the state, focusing on the institutions of violence, both political and military, as well as introducing the key concept of the civilianization of war. The second part addresses civil society at war. It asks the question as to how do men and women try to make sense and attach meaning to the violence and cruelty of war. It also explores commemoration, religious life, humanitarianism, painting, cinema and the visual arts, and war literature and testimony. The third part explores the family, gender, and migration in wartime, and shows how modern war continues to transform the world in which we live today.

Keywords: war, genocide, human rights, violence, rape

ISBNs: 9781009114271 (PB), 9781009110303 (OC)
ISSNs: 2633-8378 (online), 2633-836X (print)

Contents

Introduction
Making Sense of War

The cultural history of war overlaps with many other kinds of historical inquiry. From the mid-1960s, a robust school of social history focusing on social movements and structures contributed significantly to our understanding of twentieth-century warfare. That school drew from an earlier and equally robust school of political history, starting well before the 1914–18 war itself and continuing to this day.

Cultural history is a continuation of both of these schools of thought about war. Cultural history helps us explore the subjective experiences of war and pose the question of how men and women have made sense of the violent world in which they lived. How have they found meaning in their lives at war and in its wake? Cultural history is reflexive; it is about the construction of the historical object, war. It claims that the categories of thinking about war we use are constructs made by people who take what they have at their disposal and try to stabilize and if possible to comprehend the world at war. The language combatants and civilians use in wartime and after is rich, volatile, and part of the reality of war.

War is a fact. It is not only a system of signs but also a set of events in which people bleed and die. We know these facts only through the language in which they are expressed. Cultural historians focus on these languages and the cultural practices they disclose. They come in many forms – verbal, visual, digital, and so on. All are essential to the cultural historian.

One of the intentions of this study is to show readers how a cultural historian goes about his/her work. I do not assume readers will agree with the interpretations I offer or the answers I give to particular questions about war. But I do claim that in this Element readers will find the questions we cultural historians pose and will see how we have gone about trying to formulate answers to them.

The three-part structure of this Element reflects the way research has developed over the past fifty years of my engagement with this subject. What eighteenth-century philosophers called "civil society" pointed to the rich array of associational life spanning the space between the family and the state. This Element follows that insight. We start with the state and explore the languages different state actors use to understand and control the world of war. We then turn to the same search for meaning within civil society. Finally, we approach one area of research that has grown rapidly over the past few years: that of the family in wartime. This third domain overlaps with the first two but deserves separate treatment.

One last word about what is left out. Many subjects merit inclusion here but could not be accommodated in the space available in this format. The cultural histories of the body and of medical care are important topics that will receive separate treatment in this Elements of the History of Modern Warfare series. The subject of war veterans has important social and political aspects that must be dealt with elsewhere. The war at sea receives scant attention here; so does the world of ideas. We deal with religious practices but not enough with theology. The culture of scientific research is barely mentioned. Furthermore, there is an inevitable European bias in the discussion of the two world wars, though both were global in character. The focus on the global south in the discussion of wars after 1945 is also too limited. Of one point I am certain. The field of the cultural history of war, which has grown by leaps and bounds over the past four decades, is around to stay. Many young historians are at work today who will give new and significant answers to the questions posed in this Element.

Cultural historical approaches have been applied most widely in studies of the First World War. The bibliography attests to the richness of the literature on this period and points to the opportunity historians of warfare after 1918 have in drawing on these publications to deepen our understanding of later conflicts and how men and women have searched for meaning in them.

This is a small Element with a limited objective. Above all, the author hopes he conveys a sense of the excitement of work in this field and of his admiration for the scholarship and humanity of comrades and colleagues all over the world who have created it.

THE CULTURAL HISTORY OF THE STATE AT WAR

1 Political Culture

Political culture is the language of political power just as military culture is the language of armed forces. In the twentieth century, the instruments of power have extended well beyond an executive, Parliament, and the police to incorporate propaganda, surveillance, espionage, and thought control. The technology of eavesdropping used during the First World War was primitive compared to today's computer hacking and the fabrication of false news.

Three facets of political culture have framed warfare throughout the world over the past century. The first is cultural mobilization, or the effective deployment of a nation's cultural capital, human and institutional, in the war effort. The second is the emergence of the politics of hatred, in part because of the huge casualties caused by twentieth-century munitions, and in part because wars last for years. The will of the population to carry on has to be stiffened and the cultivation of hatred is one of the best means of doing so. The third is cultural demobilization, or the restoration of relations between adversaries and between social groups, especially (though not exclusively) in states that lose wars. In some cases, a culture of defeat leads to renewed hostilities; in others, it leads to the search for alternatives to war. In this section we examine each of these processes from a global perspective.

Cultural Mobilization

National symbols matter in wartime. Flags proliferate, and so do parades and rituals of support for the fighting men. Many of these events are organized from above, but, in some cases, popular initiatives are adopted by the state. The best instance of top-down symbolic action is the decision in 1917 of the English royal family to change its name from the all-too-German-sounding Saxe-Coburg and Gotha to Windsor, the name of their residence west of London. Towns, streets, and families followed suit all over the world. My father lived on Hamburg Street in Brooklyn during the First World War. In his books, he crossed out "Hamburg" and wrote in "Madison" in 1917, when he was twelve years old.

In Australia, the landing at Gallipoli on April 25, 1915, became Anzac Day a year after, to celebrate what Australians took to be the birth of their nation; New Zealanders did the same. In revolutionary Russia, Red Army Day was celebrated for the first time on February 23, 1919, in the midst of the Russian civil war. These instances of wartime commemoration show the strength of national feeling while the fighting was going on; such solidarity mostly came from below.

One important aspect of twentieth-century warfare is visual propaganda and the selective presentation of news. The Great War coincided with the arrival of the cinema as the centerpiece of mass entertainment around the globe; newsreels brought to the public the news the government wanted it to hear. Press offices and agencies scrambled to offer positive and hopeful accounts of wartime news in print and to block the reporting of bad news from the front.

Photographs of battlefields were cleaned up in most cases so civilians would not see dismembered bodies or severely wounded men. The same doctoring of news reports happened on all sides and on all fronts during the Second World War. One reason Churchill's speeches were so effective is that his radio audience had little idea just how vulnerable Britain was after the fall of France. Everyone in the press patriotically lied some of the time, and some lied all the time. Nazi propaganda promised a "secret weapon" would turn the tide as late as 1945.

Well before the war, the Nazi regime benefited from the brilliant cinematography of Leni Riefenstahl, Hitler's favorite cineaste. The power of the image she captured in *The Triumph of the Will* of the nation on the move gave Hitler just

Figure 1 Premier of Leni Riefenstahl's *Triumph of the Will*, Berlin, 1935.
Source: Imagno/Hulton Archive via Getty Images

what he wanted in his battle against the effete democracies of the West. In Figure 1, we see how the Nazi regime celebrated itself at the premier of Riefenstahl's film.

When Goebbels, Hitler's propaganda minister, needed to dramatize his claim that Germany was fighting against enslavement in 1945, he found the cash and the soldiers needed to act in Veit Harlan's *Kolberg*, a film about the successful German resistance against the French in 1807. The film was not shown before the collapse of the Third Reich. In Figure 2, we see Horst Caspar and Heinrich George embodying German courage in the face of foreign invasion of their country.

In recent years, television and the Internet have continued to manipulate war news. During the Iraq War of 2003–7, journalists were blocked from attending the arrival at US bases of the coffins of soldiers killed in combat. Not allowing television news reporters to cover such moments was a deliberate move to avoid the shock Americans got when they saw on TV the savagery of combat in Vietnam in the 1960s and 1970s.

The more sophisticated war became, the more a nation's "experts" mattered. The First World War was a chemist's war, the Second World War was a physicist's war, and specialists in these fields were national assets. So

Figure 2 Horst Caspar and Heinrich George in Veit Harlan's *Kolberg*, 1945.
Source: Photo by Ullstein Bild/Ullstein Bild via Getty Images

were economists and mathematicians. Every country at war mobilized its doctors and nurses. During the Second World War, the field of operations research opened up a quantitative basis for decision-making. In recent years, psychologists have been tapped to help military and civilian groups manage what is euphemistically called enhanced interrogation, or, more simply, torture. This is one dark example of the mobilization of expertise by the state at war.

Performances by great artists have embodied the nation's will to go on. On October 10, 1939, Myra Hess gave the first of her concerts at the National Gallery in the heart of London. The National Gallery, like all other museums in London, was closed, but these concerts performed the nation's will to endure no matter the cost. Dimitri Shostakovich's Symphony No. 7 was premiered on March 5, 1942, in Leningrad, halfway through the siege of the city. It is known to this day as the Leningrad Symphony.

This aspect of the cultural history of war is much more than the history of the elites' manipulation of the masses. Propaganda, produced by every combatant state, was effective only when it corresponded to the ideas and aspirations of the population as a whole. Thus it had to take into account the fact that all the organs of a nation's cultural life generate their own messages, at times under duress and surveillance, but at other times with a degree of freedom that survived all but the most savage of dictatorships.

The Cultivation of Hatred

In the twentieth century, populations at war tended to demonize the enemy and to sacralize "our" cause. Once seen in this way, the business of war becomes the destruction of evil. The downward slide from seeing adversaries as neighbors, then rivals, then enemies, then criminals, then monsters was almost inevitable. This dehumanization of the enemy was all too easy in the case of colonial and imperial warfare. Perhaps one million Chinese people were killed during popular revolts against Western domination at the turn of the twentieth century known as the Boxer Rebellion. In 1904, Kaiser Wilhelm II called on German troops to exterminate Africans who fought against German rule in southwest Africa. Up to 75 percent of the Herero population died. There is no consensus among historians as to whether this maltreatment of civilians prepared the ground for German atrocities in Belgium and northern France in 1914. Then, German troops, fearing irregular warfare from Belgian civilians, shot civilians, used them as human shields, and committed other war crimes. The Allied campaign against German atrocities emphasized their Germanness.

What the historian George Mosse described as a process of brutalization in combat was evident in colonial wars throughout the century.[1] The Rif War of the 1920s between Berber tribesmen and Spanish and French soldiers was the first war in which European troops used chemical weapons against civilians. Torture, rape, and the murder of prisoners occurred as well. This pattern of savagery recurred in all the colonial and anticolonial wars that followed. Racial prejudice made it easier to reduce the enemy below the level of a common humanity that had been affirmed by the Geneva Conventions, which we discuss in Section 7.

The racialization of warfare took a turn for the worse after the German defeat of 1918. In the aftermath, various groups led by embittered military leaders like Erich Ludendorff invented the idea that Germany had been stabbed in the back by socialists and Jews. The enemy within had snatched victory from the long-suffering German army. This legend merged with other notions that somehow the Bolshevik forces that had taken over Russia were in league with world Jewry. The putative Judeo-Bolshevik conspiracy could only be eradicated by war, and a war to the death. Why? Because they believed the Jewish danger was

---

[1] Angel Alcaide, The "brutalization thesis" (George L. Mosse) and its critics: A historiographical debate, *Pasado y memoria: Revista de historia contemporánea* (2016). DOI: 10.14198. PASADO 2016.15.01.

racial in character: Jews were evil not by choice but by nature. That is why in later years the Nazis decided every last Jewish man, woman, and child had to be wiped out.

How far is this view from the ubiquitous racism of the 1930s that turned black, brown, and yellow populations into vermin? In some places, like Britain, racial hatred took on what were termed "civilized" forms. "One" did not befriend Jews or Africans because they were likely to be money-grubbers or sexual predators. In other places, especially when anticolonial movements gathered force, the hatred between white overlords and nonwhite adversaries was even more visceral and opened the door to greater cruelty.

In the post–Second World War period, the viciousness of anticolonial warfare heightened the latent racism in all European armies engaged in "pacification" or counterinsurgency. The viciousness of the war against Japan surfaced in engagements all over Asia. Americans, for example, fought against "Chinks" in the Korean war. The Japanese army itself had displayed the same racialized brutality in its treatment of Chinese and Korean populations before and during the war.

Racism does not depend on the color of your skin; it depends on modes of thinking about a hierarchy of races and about the need to teach the lesser orders a lesson as to who they really are. The torture of Iraqi prisoners in the Abu Ghraib prison in Iraq in 2003–4 included practices inherited directly from Vietnam. Racial sadism marked many anticolonial conflicts in the period under review.

Genocide is the end point of this process of dehumanization. The extermination of the Herero people in 1904 differed from the next such case to arise in warfare, that of the Ottoman extermination of the Armenian population of Anatolia during the First World War. The difference was race, which sentenced all Hereros to death. Through marriage to Muslim men, Armenian women could and a minority did escape from the death sentence given to the entire Armenian nation for disloyalty and treachery against the Ottoman state. They could convert to Islam; more than fifty thousand did so. The Herero had no such choice, nor did the Jews during the Nazi genocide of the 1930s and 1940s.

Three other cases of genocide in the later twentieth century arose during civil wars. The Cambodian campaign of genocide under the Pol Pot regime in 1975–9 was an outgrowth of the Vietnam War, after which the regime killed more than one million of its own population. The Rwanda genocide of the Tutsi population by radical Hutus in 1994 and the genocidal treatment of Bosnian civilians by Serb paramilitary and regular forces over the period 1992–5 were alike. In both cases, one group engaged in the systematic rape and murder of another group within a state with deep ethnic divisions. The impulse to genocide could arise under circumstances other than war, but when armed conflict became racialized, then genocide became feasible.

One question still open in the cultural history of warfare is why genocide takes place in some cases and not in others. The answer seems to be that certain groups are culturally "vaccinated" against the "virus" of brutality required for participation in genocide. Through codes of honor, religious belief, or transcendental values, some people refuse to participate in collective crimes including genocide. We return to this point in our discussion of military culture.

Cultural Demobilization

The cultural historian John Horne has led the way in pointing to a cultural disengagement of forces in the aftermath of twentieth-century warfare. He has in mind the work done by many groups to find a way for those who have fought against each other for years and with heavy casualties on both sides to live together in peace. The League of Nations was founded as a site of cultural and political demobilization.[2]

After 1945, similar initiatives were launched through the United Nations (UN) and elsewhere. Many people believed the French and German populations could never live alongside each other without violence. Yet a group of leaders found a way to defuse the seventy-five years of conflict between them by constructing an economic consortium after 1950. Around the French-German pair, other nations have come to construct the European Union as it is known today.

One of the questions that preoccupies cultural historians is why that process was successful in Western Europe, given the depths of the hatred of the other in both countries. After all, the same joining together for purposes of economic recovery did not occur in East Asia. Japan and China are hardly partners; the same may be said about India, Pakistan, and Bangladesh, where war continued after the brutal struggle for decolonization from Britain.

An answer may lie in the uniqueness of the years after 1945 and the special features of European development. Partly due to the American Marshall Plan, what the French call *"les trentes glorieuses,"* the thirty wonderful years, were a time of rebirth that astonished the world. The transformation of Japanese society, stripped of its militaristic past, was equally remarkable. In other regions of military conflict, in the Middle East and in Africa, repeatedly, as well as in those countries in Latin America engaged in suppressing the political left in the

---

[2] John Horne, Demobilizing the mind: France and the legacy of the Great War, 1919–1939, *French History and Civilization*, 2 (2009), pp. 101–19.

1970s and 1980s, the warring parties did not demobilize. They kept fighting in one way or another.

The partial achievement of cultural demobilization may have been due to war crimes trials in Europe and Israel and elsewhere in truth and reconciliation commissions. The reestablishment of the principle that the rule of law exists, even in wartime, is a fundamental barrier to brutality. So was the passage of the Universal Declaration of Human Rights and the Genocide Convention in 1948, and so is the way that through various commissions, the victims of cruelty in war are given the right to speak, to tell their story, and to thereby reaffirm their humanity. The Nuremberg Trials focused more on the perpetrators than on the victims. The trial in 1961 of Adolph Eichmann in Jerusalem gave survivors a chance to tell their story. Two years later, there was a trial of Nazi personnel who served at Auschwitz. Over the next decades, similar trials took place in Germany and France. In all of them, those who suffered faced their jailers, torturers, and executioners. Without these moments of truth-telling, neither cultural demobilization nor reconciliation is possible. Giving a human face to the victim of political power may be an essential element in turning states away from war.

2 Military Culture

All armies operate through a set of rules and norms that guide a soldier's life throughout his military career. Military codes of conduct, while important, tell us much about how soldiers ought to behave. Historians study what happens to armies in wartime, not what should happen under ideal circumstances.

This field of study is one of the richest in recent historiography. Starting in the mid-1970s, historians have followed the British scholar John Keegan in asking how battle is possible. In *The Face of Battle*, Keegan defined battle as a scene of violent and terrifying danger. To escape the menace to life and limb, soldiers in medieval warfare could run to the next hill; in the nineteenth century, they could arrive a day late. From 1914 on, the level of terror accompanying men in battle rose simply because of the size and complexity of the battlefield. In effect, there was no escape from a lethal environment made infinitely more dangerous by technological change. Never before had the density of lethal particles reached such levels. Without escape, and under terrifying pressure, Keegan wrote, how is battle possible? Historians have explored many answers to this question. Many have concentrated on three elements: consent to serve, discipline, and the notion soldiers form that in combat, casualties will be proportionate to gains. Let us consider each in turn in different twentieth-century contexts.

Forming Armies: Consent to Serve

European armies had long histories before 1914. The staff work of the Prussian and then the German Imperial army was the envy of the military world. Regiments preserved their battle honors with pride. Armies had long-standing rituals and ceremonies into which new recruits were initiated. Both before and after 1945, when new countries created new armies, they had to put together their own repertoire of military rituals. The new Red Army borrowed much of its symbolic language from the tsar's army. Thirty years later, former Red Army soldiers helped create a new cultural vocabulary of military life in the Israeli army. Men and women of the new Hagganah, now the Israel Defense Forces, sang Russian songs with Hebrew verses. Even before independence, those being groomed for military careers in Africa, Asia, and South America learned what to do at the military academies of Sandhurst or Saint-Cyr. Others were schooled in ritual at West Point and other American academies and bases. Translated into different languages, a generally understood military culture was the language of the officer corps throughout the twentieth century and remains so today.

A different set of questions emerged in 1914 when mass armies had to be recruited for service "for the duration." After Christmas 1914, that meant as long as it took to win. Now the problem was how to form efficient armies and keep them staffed through the war. Population growth in the late nineteenth century provided combatants with the largest cohort of young men in history from which to choose. Although poverty reduced that cohort by a substantial percentage of men who were unable to pass the rudimentary medical standards for military service, that still left millions of able-bodied men eligible for service.

The size of armies depended primarily on the willingness of men to either volunteer or accept call-up notices. Most combatant countries conscripted their armies in both world wars. Britain until 1916, Canada until 1917, and Australia throughout the First World War operated a voluntary service. The United States began selective service in 1917; it continued until 1973.

In southern Africa, black Africans were barred from serving as combatants. Instead they were recruited to serve in the South African Native Labour Corps; six hundred of these men drowned on the way to France when the S.S. *Mendi* went down. An additional thirteen hundred Africans died on active service. The British Military Labour Bureau mobilized nearly one million porters, mostly in East Africa. Perhaps ninety-five thousand died during the war. More than one million Africans served as porters in other armies in Africa. How many died of exhaustion and disease is unknown.[3]

Impressment in the tsar's armies in Russia was widespread before 1914, and similar forms of persuasion operated wherever imperial overlords "invited" their nonwhite subjects to join up. Chinese authorities sent more than one hundred and forty thousand laborers from Shandong Province to France to help in the hard work of maintaining the Western Front. Were they volunteers? Yes. Were they exploited and maltreated? Certainly.[4]

Nevertheless, what is striking about wars in the twentieth century is how widespread was consent to service, at least in the initial stages of all major wars. Part of this can be explained as a reflection of the way military service was built into citizenship. There is little doubt that millions of men and women chose to go to war because they believed it was the right thing to do.

In many cases, those who joined up were persuaded their country was fighting a defensive war against an external enemy. Problems emerged, though, throughout the century, when wars dragged on and when casualties mounted without any sign that victory was in sight.

There were many cases of military forces formed from scratch. The new Irish National Army formed in 1922 mixed Great War soldiers with those who had fought against them after the 1916 rising. In the Spanish Civil War of 1936–9, international brigades fought on both the Nationalist and the Republican sides. All resistance groups in the Second World War had veterans in their ranks.

The vast majority of men and women who took up arms against fascism were civilians. Many were poorly trained. The Italian writer Primo Levi joined the partisans in northern Italy in 1944; this ramshackle group was quickly betrayed and arrested. As a Jew, Levi was sent to Auschwitz. Many other partisans were simply shot, since they served in irregular forces.

Men of different nationalities joined the British and French forces, just as on the other side, the Waffen-SS, the military branch of the Nazi Party's SS organization, included volunteers from many nations who served alongside German troops. Their cause was the same as that of the Nazis, in particular, the defeat of the Soviet Union and communism. For example, the 1st Cossack Cavalry Division was White Russian; the 33rd Grenadier Brigade of the SS Charlemagne Division was French; the 13th Mountain Division of the SS Handschar was composed of Bosnian and Albanian Muslims as well as

---

[3] Mahon Murphy, Carrier corps, in *1914–1918-online: International encyclopedia of the First World War*, ed. by Ute Daniel, Peter Gatrell, Oliver Janz, et al. (Berlin: Free University of Berlin, 2015). https://doi.org/10.15463/ie1418.10660

[4] Guoqi Xu, *Strangers on the Western Front: Chinese workers in the Great War* (Cambridge, MA: Harvard University Press, 2011).

Catholic Croats; and the 14th SS Volunteer Division "Galicia" was Ukrainian. They were all deemed criminal organizations after the war. The Ukrainian war cemetery in Lviv in Ukraine has graves of the men who died fighting alongside the Nazis in the Galicia Division. Next to them are the graves of Ukrainian soldiers who died fighting Russia in 2014. What these Ukrainian nationalists are saying is *la lutte continue*.

A different calculus operated with some groups of prisoners of war. Here service among former enemies meant survival for a small minority of prisoners; most starved to death. The so- called Vlasov armies were made up of Russian prisoners of war who "volunteered" to serve alongside German units. The same choice, though in the opposite direction, was made by General Friedrich Paulus, commandant of the German 6th Army. He surrendered at Stalingrad and after the unsuccessful attempt on Hitler's life in July 1944 joined the Soviet-backed National Committee for a Free Germany.

The Free India Legion was formed from Indian prisoners of war captured by Rommel's Africa Corps. Similarly the Indian National Army was formed from prisoners of war captured by the Japanese at Singapore. This force accepted the authority of Subhas Chandra Bose, who worked with Japan for Indian independence from Britain. Bose died in a plane crash after his army had been crushed in the last year of the war.

After 1945, it was difficult to speak about consent in accounts of the decision of indigenous soldiers to serve in either colonial or anticolonial forces; the same is true in the patchwork of wars that have disfigured Africa over the past fifty years. Consent is a term without meaning with respect to child soldiers. They appeared in Mozambique's civil war in 1977; thirty years later, one estimate put the number of child soldiers in Africa as one hundred and twenty thousand, with another one hundred and sixty thousand serving in Asia and Latin America.[5] Edgar, aged fourteen, shown in Figure 3, was forced to serve in the Lord's Resistance Army in Uganda in 2005. He attacked his own village. In Figure 4, we see two former child soldiers in the Sudan after their liberation by the United Nations Children's Fund (UNICEF).

Women served in combat throughout the twentieth century. The women's Battalion of Death joined in the failed tsarist offensive of July 1917 and suffered the consequences of the collapse of the Russian war effort. During the Second World War, women were conscripted and served in many capacities in the Red Army. In Britain, women were conscripted into war work but did not serve in combat units. Israeli women served alongside Israeli men from the 1948 war on.

---

[5] Claude Rakisits, Child soldiers in the east of the Democratic Republic of the Congo, *Refugee Survey Quarterly*, 27, 4 (2008), pp. 108–22, at p. 108.

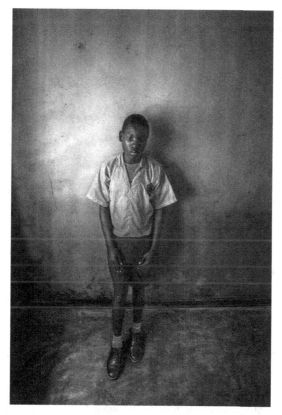

Figure 3 Edgar, fourteen, a soldier in the Lord's Resistance Army, Uganda.
Source: Photo by Alvaro Ybarra Zavala/Edit by Getty Images

Perhaps the most important role women played in war work was the way they defended and operated the supply lines on the Ho Chi Minh Trail. Women also provided essential nursing services in Asian wars just as they had done in European wars. Women played important roles in operating resistance and espionage networks under German and Italian occupation in Europe and under Japanese occupation in China, and they continued to do so after 1945. In partisan and civil wars, women played a more vital role in combat, subversion, and sabotage than they did in regular, interstate wars.

Maintaining Armies: Discipline

All armies have military police to control indiscipline; those who refuse orders risk severe punishment, even execution. In the Second World War, the German army executed more than thirty thousand men. This was one hundred times

Figure 4 Child soldiers in the Sudan, demobilized by UNICEF.
Source: Photo by Roger Lemoyne via Getty Images

greater than the number shot during the First World War. The difference between Hitler's army and that of the kaiser has no better illustration than this.

It is impossible, though, to account for the maintenance of military discipline through coercion alone. Most soldiers follow orders because they believe they are serving their nation. In wartime, a belief that victory can be achieved matters to them; so does training and drill to instill in soldiers a sense that they will respond automatically when ordered to go forward under fire. Respect for junior or non-commissioned officers who lead from the front and share the same risks as their men is important. Small-group loyalties account for the tendency of soldiers to fight for the men on their left and right in the full knowledge that they will do the same.

One important explanation for the maintenance of discipline is the preservation of ties between front and home front. Letters and food parcels express that bond and give soldiers the sense not only that their service is valued but also that they are fighting for their families. When soldiers lose touch with their home communities, they become more vulnerable to addiction to alcohol, drugs, or sex to cover their fears and their isolation. Recent research has rejected drug addiction as an explanation for the American defeat in Vietnam, but all studies of that conflict emphasize the strain on combat troops living in an environment radically different from the one they knew at home.[6]

---

[6] Jeremy Kuzmarov, *The myth of the addicted army: Vietnam and the modern war on drugs* (Boston: University of Massachusetts Press, 2009).

Proportionality

One important element to consider in studying how soldiers withstand the stress of combat is dialogue. Soldiers receive orders and attempt to carry them out, but they are not machines. They break off an engagement when they see that the costs in life and limb overwhelm any further benefit. This kind of negotiation is almost always tacit rather than explicit. Most of the time, when soldiers confront orders that are impossible to carry out without a massacre and that would yield either no gain or marginal gains, they stand down.[7]

There are examples of units going forward anyway: the Australian Third Light Horse Brigade at the Nek on Gallipoli in 1915 is one; another is the Newfoundland Regiment on the first day of the Battle of the Somme in 1916. But most of the time, it is not staff officers who issue commands but combat soldiers who decide when a military action comes to an end. That is as true today as it was one hundred years ago.

Mutiny

When men refuse to come forward or leave their units and go home, when discipline breaks down or they refuse to follow orders they believe won't lead to victory but only to more suffering and death, we say a mutiny has occurred. Many such incidents are well documented, but we should not underestimate the capacity of soldiers to subvert orders while pretending to follow them. Mutiny is what happens when morale breaks down. Lousy food, a failure to pay troops, or inadequate medical care or leave arrangements can undermine morale; so can news that suggests victory is beyond reach, and so can a privileged officer corps seen as out of touch with the ordinary fighting man.

Each of these trigger points was linked to mutiny in the First World War. Some are very well known. In May 1917, elements of the French army in rear areas refused to go back to the front. They were fed up with a command that had promised to break off engagements if a breakthrough did not occur after a certain interval. When the order to attack came even after that interval, soldiers who had already been in combat balked. The German army had no idea about this imbroglio. French soldiers were protesting against their leadership, against poor conditions. They did not call for a change of government but for a change in leadership. And that is what they got.

Two months later, in July 1917, after a futile two-week offensive on the eastern front, Russian soldiers by the thousands simply went home. The provisional government had given them the hope that they could seize land that had

---

[7] Leonard V. Smith, *Between mutiny and obedience: The case of the French Fifth Infantry Division in World War I* (Princeton, NJ: Princeton University Press, 1994).

been in the hands of the aristocracy. That is precisely what they did. In November 1917, Italian soldiers fled the lost Battle of Caporetto. They had had enough of combat.

A year later, the German navy went further and declared a mutiny not just against their commanders but also against the war and the regime that had lost it. When the order went out in early November 1918 for the German high seas fleet to seek a senseless and suicidal engagement with the British Royal Navy, sailors refused to comply. Joining radical workers, mutineers took control of the docks at Kiel. They demanded an immediate end to the war. The revolt spread throughout Germany and prepared the ground for the forced abdication of the kaiser on November 9 and the Armistice two days later.

In the Second World War, mutinies arose under similar circumstances. Around two hundred disgruntled British soldiers refused to join new units in Italy in 1943. The most serious episodes of indiscipline involved troops after the end of the war. In 1946, Indian sailors, tired of petty discrimination and lousy food, engaged in what they saw as a strike. Demonstrators in Mumbai carried the photograph of Subhas Chandra Bose, a renegade leader who had sided with the Axis powers during the war, and though the mutiny was suppressed after considerable bloodshed, it also showed that time was running out on British rule in India. In the same year, twenty thousand US troops in the Philippines took to the streets of Manila. They would obey only one order – to go home. It was, according to some authorities, the largest mutiny in US military history.[8] In Senegal in November and December 1944, a mutiny over back pay and pensions lower than those given to white soldiers led to protests and a massacre of up to three hundred Africans. In the aftermath of the killings, the French provisional government met the men's grievances.

Mutinies raise issues central to our understanding of the legitimacy of the state. As long as military leaders retain the loyalty of the men they lead, their orders carry authority. Once leaders act in ways the soldiers under their command see as unjust, unfair, or simply irresponsible, then cracks appear in the foundations of command. Those fissures can widen to the point that they bring down the whole structure of command. When generals can no longer be sure their orders will be followed, then the politicians they serve are in danger too.

The culture of mutiny is the wellspring of revolution, but not all mutinies lead to revolutions. The French army in 1917 regrouped and reasserted its authority both through courts martial and by recognizing that their men's grievances had to be heard. The Russian army in 1917 collapsed, and with it fell the provisional

---

[8] Elihu Rose, The anatomy of mutiny, *Armed Forces & Society*, 8, 4 (Summer 1982), pp. 561–74, at p. 566.

government that had decided to continue a war its people had rejected. By studying the language of mutineers, and of those who try to remind them who is in charge, we can find important clues as to the reasons some insurrections die down and others destroy entire regimes.

In some respects, the military culture of armies today (2022) is similar to those of 1914. Gone are the horses and the helmets and the plumes, but today's airborne cavalry and marines are still modeled on their earlier counterparts. As asymmetric war replaced mass war and armies slimmed down, they still faced the same problems of recruitment, discipline, and mutiny as did other armies. The motley array of criminal gangs posing as armies in some parts of the world are perhaps better understood through what can be termed criminal culture than by the military culture of the past century.

3 The Civilianization of War

Since 1914, war has changed in such a way as to erase the distinction between military and civilian targets. By the mid-twentieth century, this change meant that the overwhelming majority of casualties caused by war were suffered by civilians.

Scholars have addressed three facets of this phenomenon. The first is the emergence of concepts of total war, in which the army is defined as the cutting edge of the nation at war. Under that definition of war, everyone is a target. The second facet is the experience of revolutionary war, referring to movements aimed at the overthrow of bourgeois regimes and their replacement by communist regimes. The third is the emergence, especially after 1970, of subnational and transnational warfare in Asia, Latin America, and Africa, and its spread to Europe and North America.

Total War

The concept of total war was used widely in the latter stages of the 1914–18 conflict, but many of its features antedate the Great War. We need to look to the nineteenth century, in particular to the American Civil War, for earlier precedents. The same is true with respect to international efforts to limit the violence of war. The Geneva Conventions on the treatment of wounded soldiers and prisoners of war and the Hague Conventions on the conduct of war aimed at controlling war at precisely the time when war escaped from those limits. Humanitarian law was a partial brake on the civilianization of war, but no more than that.[9]

---

[9] Geoffrey Best: *Humanity in warfare: The modern history of the international law of armed conflicts* (London: Weidenfeld and Nicholson, 1980).

Technological change since 1900 has given states arsenals and delivery systems that have made it inevitable that the distinction between military and civilian targets in warfare would be blurred and then erased. In particular, the emergence of aerial warfare in the 1920s and 1930s and of atomic warfare in the 1940s and 1950s made warfare into the destruction, then the annihilation, either of cities or potentially of whole populations.

The power to annihilate also came of age at a time when communication and transportation systems gave to states like the Ottoman regime the power to orchestrate the deportation and murder of more than one million Armenian civilians in 1915. Railway networks and modern bureaucratic structures also gave the Nazis what they needed to execute genocide against the Jewish population of Europe.

In both cases, genocide was an answer to the question of how to deal with ethnic minorities when the survival of a multiethnic regime was at stake. Less radical solutions were found in all imperial settings. Among them was the establishment of concentration camps, beginning in the late nineteenth century in the Philippines and Cuba and continuing in southwest Africa. Enemy aliens were interned and imprisoned throughout the world during both world wars. Of the one hundred and twenty thousand people of Japanese ancestry imprisoned in the United States during the Second World War, eighty thousand were US citizens. Figure 5 shows Japanese-American families en route to internment camps in the western United States, guarded by US troops.

In the Russian empire in 1915, roughly six hundred thousand Jewish citizens of Russia were evicted from their homes on the grounds that their loyalties lay with the German and Austrian enemy facing Russian troops in Galicia and elsewhere.[10] Concentrating and uprooting ethnic minorities were wartime measures in 1914–18. Partitions in the interwar years separated ethnic groups in Upper Silesia and in Ireland. In the Second World War, the Nazis resolved the problem of multiethnicity through genocide, which is total war taken to the limits of inhumanity.

There were precedents of what we now term ethnic cleansing. Notions of total war lay behind the provisions of the treaty ending the First World War. In Lausanne in 1923, the Great Powers signed on to a population exchange agreement specifying that roughly one million Greek-Orthodox people who had fled from their homes in Anatolia thereby lost their right to live in Turkey. They could not go home again. At the same time, Greek Orthodox people still living in Turkey, save those living in Constantinople, were forcibly removed

---

[10] Peter Gatrell, War, refugeedom, revolution: Understanding Russia's refugee crisis, 1914–1918, *Cahiers du monde russe*, 58, 1–2 (2017), pp. 123–46.

Figure 5 Japanese-American families interned in the western United States in the Second World War.
Source: Photo by Hulton-Deutsch/Hulton-Deutsch Collection/Corbis via Getty Images

from their homes. On the other side of the line, approximately four hundred thousand Muslim residents of Greece were expelled forcibly from their homes and became Turkish citizens. (Only those in western Thrace were spared this.) Citizenship was thus defined in law as determined by religion. The implication was that religious minorities were hostages of the regimes in which they lived. Prisoners of war had been exchanged in war since time immemorial; this was the first time that men, women, children and the elderly were forcibly exchanged too. Under conditions of total war, human rights vanished.

The Nazi extermination of the Jews during the Second World War was an extreme case of the civilianization of war. As Inga Clendinnen showed in her classic book *Reading the Holocaust*, cultural historians have an important role to play in helping us understand both perpetrators and victims. Using insights gained in other studies of extreme violence is essential and does nothing to diminish the enormity of the Shoah.[11]

---

[11] Inga Clendinnen, *Reading the Holocaust* (Cambridge: Cambridge University Press, 2002).

Revolutionary and Counterrevolutionary War

From 1917 on, wars of social revolutionary movements, in particular the Bolshevik movement, became braided together with wars of national independence. That is, former provinces of imperial powers like Poland or Ukraine and the Baltic states waged wars against each other at the same time as they fought against the Red Army. Others, like Finland and Hungary, crushed communist insurrections. In the Russian civil war, a number of warlords aimed at the overthrow of the Bolshevik regime. They were aided by a motley arrangement of British, French, Greek, American, Canadian, Australian and Japanese soldiers; these troops did little to help the White forces and helped the Bolsheviks rally the population against Western invaders who, they claimed, were trying to restore the hold of the aristocracy on the land. If anything, Western intervention in the Russian civil war probably helped the Bolsheviks keep popular support.

Revolutionary and counterrevolutionary warfare was ugly and brutal, and entailed the starvation of populations in areas supposedly sympathetic to the enemy. Famine became an instrument of revolutionary and counterrevolutionary warfare. That is one reason the death toll in this period was a multiple of the numbers killed in combat or in captivity.

In 1936 in Spain, the forces of counterrevolution attempted to overthrow a duly elected republic. Supporting that effort in the civil war that followed were Italian and German troops and aircraft. Opposing them were volunteers from all over the world. The USSR was ostensibly on the side of the Republic, but waged war at the very same time against its ideological enemies on the left.

In the 1930s and 1940s, China was the scene of the brutal confrontation of communist and nationalist forces, which fought both against each other and against Japanese troops and their collaborators. After 1941, the Soviet Union fought for its life against the German army reinforced by collaborators from every occupied country.

These conflicts spread the ugliness of total war throughout Asia, Africa and Europe. Both the Japanese and the Germans used the grievances of subject populations in India and Ukraine, for example, to portray their war effort as one of liberation. The truth was much more complex. When the east of Europe and part of Germany were occupied by Soviet forces, they celebrated the liberation of millions from the Nazi yoke. This was both true and untrue, in that within a short period of time, these liberated areas were reoccupied and subjected to communist rule.

Total war spread to Indochina after 1945. First France, and then the United States, mistook wars of national liberation for wars of communist expansion. The death toll in these two conflicts surpassed one million people. Perhaps half a million people were killed in Indonesia in 1965–6, when the military orchestrated mass murder under the guise of destroying a communist uprising. After the end of the Vietnam War and its sequelae in 1975–80, the era of revolutionary warfare came to an end. In short order, the Soviet empire and communist regimes elsewhere collapsed from within, or, as in China, mutated to create a capitalist economy under the rule of the Chinese Communist Party. In effect, when the communist era came to an end, so did the era of total war, both for and against revolutionary regimes.

Subnational and Transnational Warfare

The end of the Cold War and the extension of globalization in the last decades of the twentieth century and after made national boundaries more porous than ever. Information, goods, capital, and people crossed national frontiers at dizzying speed. Unfortunately, the traffic in arms, drugs, and other contraband shared this transnational acceleration of trade and profit.

In place of the revolutionary/counterrevolutionary wars that had dominated the first three quarters of the twentieth century, other kinds of conflict emerged from the 1960s on. These wars were sequelae of the long and bitter struggles for independence from colonial rule all over the world. In both Congo-Brazzaville and Congo-Kinshasa, civil wars have plagued the population since independence. In the Sahel region, in the Sudan, in Burkina-Faso and Mali, in Uganda, Ethiopia, and Mozambique, armed conflicts have crippled the state and inflicted misery on the civilian populations. In Figure 6, we see Onikalit Constantine, aged thirty-eight, and his brother Onono Peter, aged forty-two, in Umyama, a camp for displaced persons in northern Uganda. Their hands were severed by the Lord's Resistance Army, who suspected them of collaboration with the Ugandan army. The genocide Hutu radicals conducted against the Tutsi population in Rwanda in 1994 is only the most extreme example of endemic violence on the African continent.

Left-wing struggles against right-wing dictatorships, many supported by the United States, transformed many parts of Latin America into war zones. From the 1960s, the Cuban revolution of Fidel Castro served as a model for other insurrectionary groups. Most failed completely. The logic of the Cold War led to American support for authoritarian regimes, even when they engaged in "dirty wars" against their own people, as in Chile and Argentina in the 1970s. Some guerrilla groups financed their efforts through narco-traffic, thereby blurring the boundary between the drug wars and political conflicts. In Mexico, the drug cartels grew so powerful that they constituted a state (or many states) within the state.

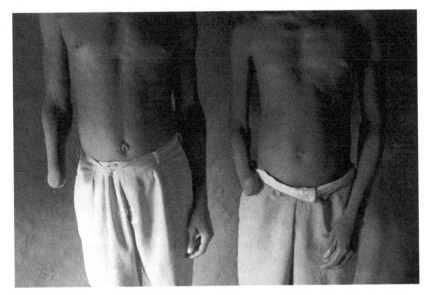

Figure 6 Onakalit Constantine, aged thirty-eight, a father of nine, stands next to his brother Onono Peter, aged forty-two, on May 27, 2005 in Umyama, a camp for displaced people in northern Uganda. Their hands were severed by the Lord's Resistance Army, who suspected them of collaboration with the Ugandan army.
Source: Photo by Per-Anders Pettersson via Getty Images

The scourge of subnational warfare is a global phenomenon. From the conflict with FARC in Colombia to the wars waged by Chechen rebels in the Caucasus to the chronic violence that flares up regularly in Gaza and the West Bank, we have seen over the past thirty years the spread of wars in which attacks upon civilians were so frequent that they took on the cloak of normality. And so did torture and extralegal killings in the waging of these wars. This is the context in which to locate the brutality of the American-led wars in Iraq and Afghanistan since 2001 and the Syrian civil war that began in 2011. They did not come out of some distinctive feature of Middle Eastern politics; they were part of a worldwide trend toward subnational violence.

The rise of radical Islam brought together transnational warfare with the savagery of domestic conflict in the Middle East. This development featured two separate facets. The first was a movement in Sunni Islam against the subjugation of Muslim nations and in particular Saudi Arabia to domination by Western states. Al-Qaeda was a transnational entity that came out of this set of ideas. The second was a parallel movement in Shia Islam to rid Iran of its Western overlords.

What ties these together is their cult of martyrdom. Suicide attacks on enemy sites always entail casualties among bystanders and other innocents, and so do retaliatory actions on behalf of the United States and its allies. In a recent trial, one of the killers who launched attacks in Paris in November 2015 said that the French government knew the risks it was taking when it participated in military action against the Islamic State in Syria. "We attacked France, targeted its population, civilians," he admitted. But, he added, "there was nothing personal."[12]

Here is the essence of the civilianization of war. Its costs are clear. We have no precise statistics of the number of civilian war-related deaths in the 1914–18 conflict. Some estimates put the total at six and a half million people, or roughly two-thirds of the total of military deaths. We have even less certainty when we turn to the mixture of revolutionary wars, national wars, ethnic wars, and brigandage in Eastern and Southern Europe in 1918–23. The ravages of epidemic disease must be taken into account. The civilian death count in these years may have been just as heavy as in the 1914–18 period. In the Second World War, civilian deaths may have constituted 50 percent of all casualties. By the end of the twentieth century, estimates of civilian deaths as a percentage of all war-related mortality vary from 50–90 percent. *Faute de mieux*, I will take the midpoint as a plausible estimate. If roughly three-quarters of all those who die in war are civilians, then we must admit that the culture of limited war – waged by armies against armies and reaching an end when one army imposes its will on the other – has faded away. In 2022, I believe, we are in a worse place than were our ancestors a century ago. The civilianization of war is a cultural phenomenon no one can ignore.

4 War and Peace

Peace is both a legal state and a state of mind. That is why no cultural history of war can afford to ignore the cultural history of the transition from war to peace and the preservation of peace thereafter.

The first point to make is that peace treaties symbolize the end of armed conflict, even when violence continues. June 28, 1919, was the date when the state of hostilities between Germany and the Allies came to an end. It was not the date when violence in Europe or elsewhere came to an end. Indeed, other treaties had to be signed to signal the end of hostilities between the Allies and the Central Powers. The final treaty in this series was signed on July 24, 1923, in

---

[12] Paris attacker rants in trial that France "knew risks" of striking jihadists in Syria, France 24, September 15, 2021. www.france24.com/en/france/20210915-paris-attacker-rants-in-trial-that-france-knew-risks-of-striking-jihadists-in-syria

Lausanne, between Turkey and the Allies. In the period 1919–23, war continued in a huge arc from Finland to Turkey because the collapse of empires and the Russian Revolution fueled wars of national independence and revolution in many countries. War bled into peace for four years; millions of lives were lost in this transitional moment.

Only then could a process that the historian John Horne termed cultural demobilization gather momentum. Horne focuses on language and images that separated Verdun, the quintessential battlefield, from Locarno, the quintessential site of peacemaking, where former enemies embrace and declare their commitment to a lasting peace.[13] In other words, the peace process lasted long after the formal end of hostilities. Only when former adversaries were prepared to make sacrifices for peace could they leave behind their sacrifices for war.

The biggest sacrifice for peace attempted during the twentieth century was absolute state sovereignty. That is what was at stake in the founding of the League. The Covenant of the League of Nations stipulated that the High Contracting Bodies accept three fundamental obligations: first, not to resort to war; second, to make international law the basis for "the actual rule of conduct" among governments; and third, to maintain justice and a scrupulous respect for treaty obligations.[14] Each of these commitments reduced the absolute freedom of states to protect their national interests as they saw fit.

This document, signed on June 28, 1919, was revolutionary in character. Nothing like it had accompanied peace treaties in the past. The problem, though, to which no one found a solution, was that every state compromised its absolute sovereignty only in theory and not in practice. Time and again, individual states found ways to bypass their commitments to peace, to law, and to justice. In other words, cultural demobilization was only skin deep. The essence of state power remained intact.

The League did make a lasting contribution to peace in another way. Its auxiliary organizations, including the International Labour Organization and the World Health Organization, established rules for the defense of the working conditions and health of populations all over the world. These measures became norms that have lasted to this day. In addition, the League operated Mandates that prepared colonies and dependencies for independence, thereby starting the clock ticking on the end of direct imperial rule.[15]

---

[13] John Horne, Demobilizing the mind, French civilization and culture. https://h-france.net/rude/wp-content/uploads/2017/08/vol2_Horne_Final_Version.pdf

[14] For the original text, see, for example, the French official document, www.senat.fr/histoire/le_banquet_wilson/traite/covenant_of_the_league_of_nations.html.

[15] Susan Pedersen, *The Guardians: The League of Nations and the crisis of empire* (New York: Oxford University Press, 2017).

What was most significant about the League was its effort, albeit unsuccessful, to creative a general category of collective security in the interests of which states would sacrifice a part of their sovereignty. As we have noted, John Horne cited the treaties of Locarno in 1925 as examples of this effort; in these agreements, the major powers, including Germany, promised to recognize and respect the borders of their neighbors. Three years later, on August 27, 1928, representatives of Germany, France, and the United States signed the Treaty for the General Renunciation of War As an Instrument of National Policy. Subsequently, another forty states signed on. It is important to note that these two agreements were not promulgated by the League of Nations, but were signed outside of the League by independent states. Here we see proof positive of the survival of sovereignty as the ultimate measure of foreign policy.

The decade-long peace process that spanned the period from the signing of the Covenant of the League of Nations to the signing of the Kellogg-Briand Pact was ended by the world economic crisis of 1929–31. Over the turbulent decade that followed, it became apparent that economic instability bred political instability, and that with the accession to power of the Nazi Party in 1933, there would be a reversion to the absolute primacy of national authority over collective security. In 1938, when the future of Czechoslovakia, one of the original signatories of the Covenant of the League, was in the balance, the League failed to defend international law and justice. Instead, Britain, France, Italy, and Germany ran roughshod over the League and crucified Czechoslovakia. In Figure 7, we see Hitler greeted by triumphant German crowds after his diplomatic triumph in Munich in 1938.

First the Sudetenland, then the rest of the Czech lands, were occupied by the Nazis while the newly "independent" Slovakia became a puppet state. After the Second World War, the UN established a second platform as a means of continuing the search for collective security. The UN's Human Rights Commission also drafted the Universal Declaration of Human Rights, which was unanimously accepted by the UN members meeting in Paris on December 10, 1948. The thought behind this document was clear: states that violated the rights of their own citizens sooner or later violated the territory of their neighbors. To defend human rights was to fortify the peace.[16] In this declaration, there was no mention of the right of subject peoples to fight for freedom. In 1976, the UN rectified this omission in its International Covenant on Civil and Political Rights and International Covenant on Economic, Social and Cultural Rights.

---

[16] Jay Winter and Antoine Prost, *René Cassin: From the Great War to the Universal Declaration* (Cambridge: Cambridge University Press, 2012).

Figure 7 Hitler greeted by crowds after his diplomatic
triumph in Munich in 1938.
Source: Photo by Bettmann via Getty images

Nevertheless, the end of the era of empires in the twentieth century did not resolve the conflict between the sovereignty of nation-states and the authority of the UN to defend the peace. The UN Security Council acted to defend the peace in Korea in 1950, but only after the Soviet Union had walked out of its proceedings. In later years, one or another of the permanent members blocked collective action when their national interests or those of their allies came into play. Consequently, various peace processes underway to resolve regional conflicts had to bypass the logjam of the UN. Since there have been very few conflicts on which the great powers agree, the UN has not been able to staunch the bloodbath in long-running conflicts like the Syrian civil war.

How does a cultural historical approach help us understand the enduring power of state sovereignty to resist collective solutions to armed conflict? The choice between war and peace is both rational and emotional; what the cultural historian James Joll called the unspoken assumptions leaders developed long before 1914 about honor and dignity help us see why statesmen reacted in the way they did.[17] Both world wars were fought to defend the sovereignty of weak states invaded by strong ones: Belgium in 1914 and Poland in 1939. Both world

---

[17] James Joll, *1914: The unspoken assumptions* (London: London School of Economics, 1968).

wars were also struggles among the powers for European and world hegemony. Consequently, other emotions came into play, emotions of which we can find traces in diaries, letters, and images. The bitterness these wars cultivated in populations all over the world made it very difficult for what Horne termed cultural demobilization to take place. And without a degree of intellectual and emotional disengagement of forces over a considerable period of time, the seeds of amity planted by individuals and groups could not germinate and emerge in the light of day. The outbreak of war in 1939 was not greeted by joy in the capitals of Europe. Why? Because everyone knew what was coming. They had seen it before, and they had failed to stop the return of the nightmare. Here was a failure with a history overloaded with images, sounds, fears, and missed opportunities.

In the later twentieth century, a new kind of war crimes trial emerged. It was not the holding to account of the vanquished by the victors of international war. It was a time of reckoning with the crimes of internal wars waged by dictators over their own people. Its aim was domestic cultural demobilization.

In some cases, the impulse behind these proceedings was religious. The work of Bishop Desmond Tutu to provide a Christian core to the South African Truth and Reconciliation Commission of 1996 is well known. In Figure 8, we see

Figure 8 Leader of South Africa's National Party Frederik de Klerk (left) shakes hands with the head of the Truth and Reconciliation Commission (TRC), Archbishop Desmond Tutu, prior to presenting the submission of the National Party at the TRC offices in Cape Town, May 14, 1996.
Source: Photo by Anna Zieminski/AFP via Getty Images

Bishop Tutu shaking hands with President Frederik de Klerk of South Africa before de Klerk gave evidence to the Commission.

The Christian pathway of confession, repentance, and forgiveness enabled those who tortured and killed the enemies of apartheid to be confronted by their victims, their families, and their nation. It enabled them to confront themselves. Speaking the truth and only the truth set free approximately fifteen hundred of them.

A number of Latin American nations publicly exposed the war authorities waged against their own people in the later twentieth century. Tribunals sat in Argentina, Chile, Colombia, Ecuador, El Salvador, and Uruguay. African nations organized similar truth commissions in Algeria, Chad, the Democratic Republic of the Congo, the Gambia, Kenya, Rwanda, Sierra Leone, and Togo. In Europe, crimes under communist rule were the subject of proceedings in the Czech Republic, Germany, and Poland. The president of Yugoslavia set up a truth and reconciliation committee in 2001 to examine crimes committed during the wars in the 1990s in that country. When that state was formally dissolved in 2003, the commission ceased to exist. There is little evidence of reconciliation in that still war-torn country today (2022).

The jury is still out as to whether such commissions helped reduce internecine tensions in states marked by earlier periods of extended violence. The same doubts persist as to whether the workings of the International Criminal Court in the Hague offer what is now termed transitional justice, helping to pave a pathway to peace and democracy. To many people, the most important element in these proceedings is that those who have suffered violence have been given a right to be heard. Giving victims a voice in these proceedings is a way of helping them restore their dignity and their authority over their own lives. What is less clear is whether such tribunals inoculate these populations against the urge to return to domestic or international violence.

Cultural demobilization does happen; who would have imagined in 1945 that traffic in 1995 would pass between France and Germany as easily as between England and Wales? And yet in other places, under other conditions, hatreds and resentments burn on. Remembering injustice can put further obstacles in the way of reconciliation. Recalling injury may not provide the grounds for forgiveness. Memory is neutral; those who see it as therapeutic are frequently disappointed. To a degree, to bet on peace is an act of faith. It is to believe that the future need not repeat the past.

Cultural historians can help us see how people in the past have framed the choice between war and peace. From them we can learn as much about why peace initiatives collapse as about why war efforts collapse. To believe that war is built into our genome is intellectual nonsense. War is always a choice made by groups of people for multiple reasons. And so is peace. One way to understand the persistence of violent conflicts around the globe is as a collective failure of nerve, of courage, of imagination. Historians can help us understand that failure, and may even help us overcome it someday. War, like peace, is a choice about matters on which cultural historians have something to say. To paraphrase French premier Clemenceau, war and peace are too serious a matter to be left to the political and military historians alone.

THE CULTURAL HISTORY OF CIVIL SOCIETY AT WAR

5 Commemoration

Remembrance is a process, memory its product. Commemoration is remembrance in public. Commemorative acts happen during wartime and long after the end of hostilities. The groups that prepare and conduct these events come from all social strata. What they do is frequently in dialogue with state officials, though the initiatives they take arise overwhelmingly from civil society.

In authoritarian regimes such as the USSR under Stalin or Hitler's Germany, civil society is either damaged or silenced. In these cases, the freedom of small groups of people who do the work of remembrance is severely curtailed. In most other societies, though, commemoration is a bottom-up affair. Design, finance, orchestration, and repetition of earlier ceremonies are all the work of memory agents – people who take the time and make the effort to make commemoration happen. Without them, commemorative events cease and commemorative sites crumble or fade away.

The Lost Generation

What made commemoration both necessary and ubiquitous was the exponential rise in the number of soldiers who died in combat in the twentieth century. Approximately ten million soldiers died of war-related causes between 1914 and 1918; twice that number of soldiers perished in the 1939–45 war, but at least thirty million civilians also died in the conflict. The civilianization of war continued after 1945. At least half and probably much more than half of all war-related deaths since 1945 have been those of civilians.

Mass death in warfare was a function of technology. Artillery fire in the First World War and strategic bombing in the Second World War obliterated the enemy. Consequently, in both world wars, at least 50 percent of those who died had no known graves. How to grieve those who died and whose bodies vanished was a perennial question during and after the two world wars. In all combatant countries, war cemeteries were filled with the remains of those who could be identified and of thousands of unidentifiable bodies. As we see in Figure 9, the remains of bodies without names were dignified simply as unknown "Soldiers of the Great War" or as those whose names are known only to God.

Commemoration provided the burial ceremonies denied all too frequently to the families of those who died in wartime. The civilianization of war made military ceremonies of little use to populations at large. Instead, throughout the world new and striking ceremonies emerged from within civil society itself. In towns across the globe, committees of civilians, usually too old to serve, were formed to carry through a project of remembrance. In thousands of cases, the key to these commemorative sites was their listing of the names of those who had died. This makes perfect sense in the light of the disappearance of the missing and presumed dead. All that remained of them were their names. And given the fact that with a few exceptions, all armies conscripted those who served, the Lost Generation was composed of a cross-section of the whole society at war. Mass death democratized commemoration, leading to the listing of names alphabetically in most cases rather than by rank. That is what statues and plaques and obelisks did: they provided space for the names of the fallen.

In most cases, ordinary people paid for these war memorials. They had to get planning permission or satisfy local officials in other ways, then find a sculptor or stonemason or both, and choose a design. Mail-order catalogues were available for those who wanted to imitate the neighbors, but committee-men and women at times had very specific ideas as to what was appropriate.

Figure 9 An unknown soldier of the Great War, Commonwealth War Graves Cemetery, Ypres, Belgium.
Source: Carmen Martinez Torron via Getty Images

Once erected in crossroads or other venues, these monuments became what Pierre Nora has termed sites of memory. They were permanent additions to the landscape of towns and villages because every year on specified dates ceremonies were held there to honor the dead. Some of these ceremonies were held in city cemeteries. In Figure 10, we see a sculpture placed in the Mirogoj cemetery in Zagreb. It shows a mother holding her dead child, a Pietà, representing Croat soldiers who died fighting for Austria-Hungary in the Great War.

In the interwar years, these sites were places for women to enter directly into the narrative of war service and sacrifice. Mothers or widows in black had privileged places in these ceremonies, as did veterans and their flags. In France, as Antoine Prost noted, the flags were lowered before the dead.[18] In other countries, the flags remained where they were, suggesting, as George Mosse put it, that these were places for the worship not of the dead but of the state for which they died.[19] In both democracies and dictatorships, the dead were present among the living. For some people, remembering them served to make another war unthinkable; for others, it made another war necessary.

The Second World War and After

For many of the nations that had fought the Great War, commemorating the Second World War was problematic. Part of the difficulty was economic. Most countries had suffered considerably during the world economic crisis and found themselves in economic difficulties after a war in which they had invested, if not all, then almost all, of their resources. For this reason alone, many lists of names of those who died in the Second World War were simply affixed to existing war memorials. In churches and schools, a second plaque was added alongside the ones listing First World War dead. Among defeated populations, such lists of the dead appeared in churches. But in Germany, Italy, and Japan, as well as in occupied countries where collaboration was a painful issue, there was less public commemoration of those who died on military service.

In many countries, though, especially in Asia, the Second World War was not at all a rerun of the First. The Soviet Union commemorated not the First World War but the Bolshevik Revolution of 1917, and so did its satellite states. In contrast, in the Western European and Atlantic worlds, First World War commemorative forms and practices, local in character and somber in form, persisted after 1945.

---

[18] Antoine Prost, The impact of war on French and German political cultures, *Historical Journal* (1994), pp. 128–54.

[19] George Mosse, *Fallen soldiers: Reshaping the memory of the world wars* (Oxford: Oxford University Press, 1990), p. 236.

Figure 10 Monument to Croat soldiers who died in the Great War, Mirogoj
cemetery, Zagreb, Croatia.

Source: Filip Hameršak

The Soviet Union created heroic monuments to the dead of the Great Patriotic
War very different from those erected in Western Europe. Many are larger than
life, and some are gigantic. The statue of the Motherland calling her people to
battle in Stalingrad is 85 metres high. In 1967, the Soviet Union followed
Western practice in placing the Tomb of the Unknown Soldier of the Second
World War in the Kremlin wall.

The term *Holocaust* is a Greek term meaning a fiery offering to the gods in
which the whole of the sacrificed animal is consumed by flame. German soldiers
in the First World War used that term for the artillery war. The two terms used to
connote the Nazi genocide against the Jews are *Holocaust* and *Shoah*. Many
people object to the term *Holocaust* on the grounds that there was nothing
sacred about genocide. *Shoah* means a catastrophe. We use the term *Shoah*
throughout.

It took roughly twenty-five years before public opinion in Western Europe
accepted the fact that the Shoah was not only an essential part of the Second
World War but a unique catastrophe. What was different was its assembly-line
character and its relentlessness. Colonial atrocities followed the logic of racial
exploitation; Nazi atrocities followed the logic of racial murder, that of killing

every single person of the targeted population. By the 1980s, archives and commemorative sites to victims of the Shoah proliferated in Germany and in the rest of the Atlantic world, but not in Eastern Europe or Russia, where most of the killings took place. Soviet officials did not commemorate the Shoah as such; to them, as in the case of Babi Yar near Kiev, monuments marked one more Nazi crime against humanity. Communist Poland commemorated the uprising of the Warsaw ghetto in 1943 as a heroic act of defiance, like many others. The war against the Jews was part of the war against "the people" in the slogan of the day.

We should not generalize the history of commemoration of the Shoah from the statements of state officials. Other kinds of commemoration were organized. Individuals who returned to the Soviet Union followed traditional Jewish practice in writing what were called "Yizkor books" or commemorative accounts of particular individuals or groups.[20] The same genre grew rapidly in Israel, where many families honored in such books the six thousand Jewish dead in the 1947–8 war of independence.[21]

Commemoration of the Second World War in Asia and the Pacific followed a different trajectory. For decades, the heroic struggle of the Chinese Communist Party against Chinese nationalists and then against the Japanese was told in black-and-white terms. In recent years, though, and in local museums, the role of the nationalist Kuomintang in the defense of China during the 1930s and 1940s has been acknowledged.[22] Such developments reflect the foreign policy needs of the Chinese government.

The presentations by the North Korean government of the war of 1950–3, and of the Vietnamese government of the war against first France and then the United States, show fewer signs of accepting the color grey instead of the older black-and-white narrative of good against evil. But even when the party line is clear, at the local level, forms of commemoration exist, as it were, below the level of the Communist Party's radar. As Heonik Kwon has shown, the party ignored totally the crucial role women played in the underground supply line known as the Ho Chi Minh Trail. Using older cultural forms, in particular ghost stories, ordinary people have framed a commemorative language that highlights tragedy rather than heroism and that incorporates women's stories in the

---

[20] Mordechai Altschuler, Jewish Holocaust commemorative activity in the USSR under Stalin, Yad Vashem, Shoah Resource Center. www.yadvashem.org/odot_pdf/Microsoft%20Word%20-% 205422.pdf

[21] Emmanuel Sivan, Yizkor books and commemoration in Israel in 1948, in *War and remembrance in the twentieth century,* ed. by Jay Winter and Emmanuel Sivan (Cambridge: Cambridge University Press, 1999), pp. 168–95.

[22] Rana Mitter, *China's good war: How World War II is shaping a new nationalism* (Cambridge, MA: Harvard University Press, 2020).

national war narrative. The subtle tales of restless spirits are far from a Communist Party tract.[23] Kwon has broken new ground too in showing how survivors of the Korean War in both the north and the south have used traditional stories and rituals to piece together narratives of their families.[24]

There are striking parallels between the changing balance of war narratives in China and Korea and those that have developed in Japan since the Second World War. What the state says and what happens below the level of the national move in different directions. Officially, in 2001, the Japanese government accepted responsibility for the suffering it brought about in the Second World War.

A visit to the semiofficial Yasukuni shrine in Tokyo tells another story. This Shinto shrine, opened in 1869, honors all those who died for the emperor in wars between then and 1954. All are sanctified for their sacrifice. These men were not martyrs but loyal servants of the emperor. Adjacent to the shrine is the Yushukan War Memorial museum. It includes photographs and biographies of Japanese men who died for their country. We learn that many loved to play baseball. Narratives in the museum blame the Chinese and the West for the war and play down Japanese brutality during it. In front of the museum is a statue of a defiant kamikaze pilot, placed there in 2005 near a list of five thousand men who died in aerial suicide missions. Not far away is a statue of Indian jurist Radha Binod Pal, who dissented from the judgment of the court and found innocent all the Japanese military men tried before the International Military Tribunal for the Far East.

Second World War commemoration is still an explosive subject in Asia. What matters for us is that even this brief survey suffices to show that is it unwise to locate the history of war commemoration solely in official language. There is today and has been for some time an active and ongoing dialogue in which civil society plays a vital and multifaceted role.

After the Cold War

One way to understand the proliferation of war memorials in the period since 1989 is to see them as palimpsests. That is, older monuments have been removed, rededicated, or affixed with new meanings, and new monuments have emerged to highlight stories eclipsed during the communist era. This transition is particularly evident in the Mirogoj cemetery in Zagreb. Buried there are French, Italian, and Serb soldiers who died in the First World War.

---

[23] Heonik Kwon, *Ghosts in Vietnam* (Cambridge: Cambridge University Press, 2004).
[24] Heonik Kwon, *After the Korean War: An intimate history* (Cambridge: Cambridge University Press, 2020).

There too is a German war cemetery. After 1945, the graves of German soldiers and their Ustaše allies were effaced. After the end of the Yugoslav civil war, the *Volksbund Deutsche Kriefsgäberfürsorge*, a voluntary organization that cares for German war cemeteries, restored the German graves. Only one family has placed a cross on the grave of an Ustaše soldier; the rest remain covered by a single plaque. Nearby is a Pietà covering a mass grave of soldiers who died in the 1914–18 war. The official dedication has it that these are Croat soldiers. More recent research has shown that the remains lie there of many other nationalities. An explanatory sign provides details.

Among other prominent monuments in this cemetery are three worthy of comment in this discussion. The first is to Croats, for the large part civilians, who tried to flee the partisans in 1945 and find sanctuary with the American or British armies. They were handed back to Tito's forces. The second is a monument to the victims of what Croats refer to as the Patriotic War of 1992–5. The third is to victims of the Shoah. In this one commemorative site, we have layer upon layer of commemorative activity, each speaking to the need to remember the horrors of war. What we do not have is a single narrative.

And perhaps that is right and proper. States don't remember; people do, typically in small groups. Even when a dictatorship tries to create a unified story about war, usually one that justifies its hold on power, it rarely succeeds. Family stories and individual initiatives trump political dogma. Different groups find their voices at different times. Commemoration is everybody's business. That is why polyphony is the music of remembrance.

6 Religious Life and War

In this section, we examine a proposition in comparative cultural history. It is that the cultural history of religious institutions and beliefs in wartime can be understood best as a clash between the political framework in which churches operate and the universal ideas they profess. War is, as Clausewitz said, politics by other means. Hence when the political necessities of war appear, they tend to dominate or deform the ideas that express religious faith. There are, to be sure, exceptions to this rule. But over the twentieth century, all religious communities have had to confront or make compromises with those in power. In this chapter of the cultural history of war, each religious community has its own story to tell. Let us start with the Christian world before turning to Islam and then to the Jewish world. In conclusion we offer a few words about nonviolence in Buddhism and Hinduism.

The Christian World

The outbreak of war in 1914 and the terrible casualties of the first months of the conflict put on the shoulders of the clergy a heavy responsibility. They needed to reassure their parishioners that their cause was just, that God was by their side, that those who had died had given their lives to defend their country. Those who had any doubts as to the veracity of any one of these affirmations kept their peace. Chaplains accompanied those mobilized on their road to battle and on their road back again, at the front, in the hospital, back at home. In Germany, Austria, Britain, Italy, and France, rabbis played the same role as priests or pastors. They ministered to their men.

The bloodbath of the first year of the war was so huge that propaganda transformed the conflict into one of good versus evil. The sacralization of the conflict was announced on both sides and from every denominational pulpit. Churchmen, whether they liked it or not, had to be propagandists for the national cause.

In 1915, an older trope emerged in religious language on the Allied side. The Ottoman Turkish government took a decision to deport from Anatolia its Armenian population, whom they suspected of siding with its enemy Russia. Deportation in this case meant genocide. Men, women, and children forced from their homes were set upon immediately. The men were killed, thousands of women were raped, and the survivors were forced to survive without food and water in the Mesopotamian desert. More than one million innocent people died as a result of this deportation order.

Russian diplomats urged their colleagues to issue an official protest. This crime was an outrage against Christianity and civilization, the Russians said, echoing older campaigns protesting Turkish atrocities in the nineteenth century. In 1915, the Allies were mindful of the opinion of Muslims and Hindus who lived under British and French rule, but who would be offended by diplomatic language referring to the offense as one against Christianity alone. In many countries were hundreds of thousands of Muslim soldiers who had fought in the Indian and French armies. Instead, the Allies urged all to protest against the barbaric treatment of the Armenian people as a crime against humanity. Thus diplomatic language adapted to a war effort that included large populations of Muslims and Hindus.

The role of the Vatican in wartime diplomacy disclosed the limits of church power. The Catholic community in the Austro-Hungarian empire was no less important to Pope Benedict XV than were the Catholics of Belgium and France. The fact that the pope did not denounce Germany for the destruction of churches and the killings of churchmen in the early months of the war made it impossible for the pope to occupy a mediator's position between the two sides. Papal peace initiatives throughout the war got nowhere.

The Russian Revolution of 1917 changed the war and the peace. After the Armistice, multiple national and civil wars broke out in what some historians call the shatter-zones of empire. The Red Army invaded Poland and was only turned back in October 1920. Western intervention helped here, but not elsewhere. Thus independent Poland and the Baltic states faced the Soviet Union in an armed truce for twenty years. In this confrontation, the Catholic Church spoke for the people. In Russia itself, the Orthodox Church was forced underground, and, in Hungary in 1919, the short-lived communist regime broke up religious celebrations by force. For Armenians, their church embodied and spoke for the nation. When Bolsheviks took over independent Armenia in the Caucasus in 1920, the church kept the national cause alive throughout the diaspora.

Anticommunism informed the attitude of Catholic parties and the Vatican in the interwar years. In 1933, Cardinal Pacelli, later Pope Pius XII, negotiated the Concordat with the new Nazi regime. The Nazis promised to leave untouched Roman Catholic education; in return, the Vatican persuaded the Catholic Centre Party to dissolve itself. This step was part of the Vatican's commitment to stop the political activity of priests.

The same conflicts over anticommunism had colored the role of Catholics in the Spanish Civil War, which lasted from 1936 to 1939. There were Catholics in the Republican camp, especially in the northern Basque region. Left-wing militants desecrated churches and cemeteries and took the lives of approximately seven thousand priests and other religious in the war. In Figure 11, we see the desecration of sarcophagi in the Concepción monastery in Toledo, Spain, in 1936. The majority of Spanish Catholics ultimately sided with Francisco Franco and his nationalist forces, who declared victory on April 1, 1939.

An anti-Nazi group emerged among German Protestants within days of the Nazi seizure of power. They rejected the Prussian church's decision to adopt "the Aryan paragraph" preventing men of Jewish descent who had converted to Protestantism to act as priests. This undermined the core belief of Protestants that salvation was by faith alone. A number of clergymen, including Martin Niemöller, a former U-boat commander, and Dietrich Bonhoeffer, a theologian with strong international connections, helped steer this group into what became known as the Confessional Church (*Bekennende Kirche*). At Barmen in 1934, these rebels insisted that the church belonged not to the state but only to God. In 1937, Niemöller was arrested; he remained in prison until 1945. Bonhoeffer, who was in the outer circle of the group

Figure 11 Desecration of sarcophagi in the Concepción monastery, Toledo, Spain, 1936.
Source: Photo by Heinrich Hoffmann/Ullstein Bild via Getty Images

plotting Hitler's assassination in 1944, was executed just before the end of the war.

After 1939, Nazi military victories placed the Christian churches in occupied countries in a difficult position. Churchmen were there to protect their flock, but to do so, would they have to keep silent in the face of Nazi barbarity? Each churchman or member of a religious order, like each churchgoer, made up his or her own mind about this question. There is considerable dispute as to whether the Vatican tilted toward the Nazi side during the war in order to prevent a Soviet takeover of Europe. Even more heat is generated in arguments as to whether the pope was indifferent to the fate of the Jews. Pius XII was a diplomat used to working through indirection and official silence. The Vatican did help save the lives of some Italian Jews, but, unlike churchmen in many occupied countries, the pope never openly condemned the Nazis' anti-Semitic program.

In one case, the Vatican almost certainly knew about the barbarities practiced by the Ustaše collaborationist regime in Croatia. The Ustaše leader Anton Pavelić had a private audience with the pope in May 1941. They met again in 1943. Between these meetings, the Ustaše unleashed a genocidal campaign against Jews and Orthodox Serbs. Vatican officials and contacts did work to save Jewish lives in Croatia. Archbishop Stepinac himself denounced Ustaše violence against Jews and saved Jewish lives. Pacelli was trying to strike a compromise between Pavelić and Stepinac. The pope's critics believe that he tolerated Croat nationalism as a bulwark against communism. On one hand, the Vatican protested against deportations from Slovenia in 1943; on the other hand, the pope blocked denunciations of Croat priests who had taken part in the killings. By leaving so many grey areas in its wartime diplomacy, the Vatican sowed the seeds of a controversy still alive today. Now that the Vatican archives for this period are open to research, we may learn more about this story in the coming years.

In every occupied country, clergymen faced similar dilemmas. In France, one of the worst wartime collaborators, Paul Touvier, disappeared when the Germans withdrew from France in 1944. He spent the next forty years living incognito in a series of Catholic monasteries, protected by different church orders. So-called ratlines offered high Nazi officers a pathway to South America, according to some, with the full knowledge of the Vatican.[25]

A similar controversy follows the present pope, Francis. As a Jesuit priest in Argentina during the Dirty War, he tried and failed to liberate two fellow priests who were arrested and tortured. His critics do not claim that he denounced anyone or worked with the secret police. They say that he did not speak out openly. Shades of Pius XII? Or silence laced with innocence? Who is to say? In most of the social conflicts in Latin America and Africa, priests have been on both sides. Some took the position of liberation theology. The church, these people said, had to have a preference for the poor. It had to speak for those who had nothing or not speak at all. Others sided with the authorities. When international war mutated into subnational or civil wars after 1945, the ugliness of violence defaced both sides. In such a world, churchmen are no different from anyone else. They grope for answers in the dark.

The Muslim World

In November 1914, Sultan Mehmed V issued a *fatwa*, or formal legal ruling, that Ottoman Turkey was engaged in a holy war, a *jihad*. This act was intended to

---

[25] Philippe Sands, *The Ratline Love, lies and justice on the trail of a Nazi fugitive* (London: Weidenfeld and Nicolson, 2020).

Figure 12 *Jihad* pronounced, Fatih mosque, Constantinople, 1914.
Source: Photo by The Print Collector via Getty Images

mobilize the Muslim population of the empire, and in particular those parts of the empire in what is now Egypt, Saudi Arabia, and Palestine targeted by the British, to undermine the Ottoman regime. *Jihad* was no call to create a global Muslim empire but an appeal to Muslim public opinion to stand by the sultan.[26] In Figure 12, we see the pronunciation of *jihad* at the Fatih mosque in Constantinople.

During the war there were mutinies in Aden and Singapore as well as an uprising in the Punjab, indicating that not all Muslims were unequivocal supporters of the Allied cause. The impact of war on Islam was significant in the 1920s too. After the victory of Turkey in the Greek-Turkish conflict, the leader of the Grand National Assembly in Ankara, Mustafa Kemal, abolished both the sultanate and the caliphate. His severing of Turkey from the holy places of Islam left open the question as to who had authority over them. In addition, many Muslims were appalled by the behavior of Egypt's leaders, so subservient to their British overlords. Under these circumstances, in 1928, a group of conservative Muslims met in Cairo and created a new organization, the Muslim Brotherhood. Their leader, Hassan al-Banna, a schoolteacher, believed that a return to the Koran would enable Egyptians to restore their dignity.

---

[26] Mustafa Aksakal, "Holy war made in Germany?" Ottoman origins of the 1914 *jihad*, *War in History*, 18, 2 (April 2011), pp. 184–99.

His small movement grew rapidly and became a focus of opposition, particularly among the poor. Al-Banna was not anti-Western, just anticolonial. The Muslim Brotherhood supported the Palestinian national movement and organized a boycott of Jewish shops in Cairo because its members believed they were supporting the Zionist cause. Later, al-Banna rejected completely the nationalism of fascist Italy and Germany. Whether his organization received funding from either country is still an open question. In 1948, he supported sending volunteers to fight against Israel. In December of that year, the Brotherhood was banned and its assets impounded. On February 12, 1949, al-Banna was killed by unknown gunmen. Rumors circulated that King Farouk was behind the killing.

That is by no means the end of the story. On October 6, 1981, Anwar Sa'adat, the third president of Egypt, was assassinated. The assassins were caught and tortured, and most of them were executed. The transcript of their interrogation makes enlightening reading. Members of the Muslim Brotherhood, including Ayman al Zawahiri, a former doctor and now the ostensible head of al-Qaeda, engaged in a learned theological discussion with their interrogators. Why did they kill Sa'adat? Everyone knew that the Koran enjoined devout Muslims to obey the prince. The prisoners cited an influential member of the Muslim Brotherhood, Sayyid Qutb, who had been hanged for treason in Egypt in 1966. Qutb had argued that the only justification for regicide was when it was one minute to midnight before the destruction of Islam. That is, a tyrant could be overthrown if his actions threatened the integrity or indeed the future existence of Islam itself. He supported his views by citing a medieval Muslim theologian, Ibn Taymiyyah.[27] Making peace with Israel was not the reason Sa'adat was murdered. That act may have been number nine or ten on the assassins' bill of indictment. The real reason he was killed was that, by giving women a fuller place within Egyptian society, he had threatened the integrity of the Muslim family, which (in their view) endangered Islam itself. Thus the assassins of Saadat and the followers of al-Qaeda both took up arms in extremis.

They carried forward the same struggle of the Muslim Brotherhood to find a moral core for the Islamic world in the vacuum created by the failed peace after the First World War. It is telling that while Mustafa Kemal Ataturk had abolished the caliphate in 1924, nearly a century later, the radical Muslim group Isis attempted to resurrect it. The echoes of the past are still audible in today's religious violence.

---

[27] Emmanuel Sivan, *Radical Islam: Medieval theology and modern politics* (New Haven, CT: Yale University Press, 1985).

The Jewish World

Jewish soldiers fought in most combatant armies during the Great War. That in itself was a major step toward Jewish assimilation, a dream that had emerged during the French Revolution. In addition, Zionist organizations had won, in the Balfour Declaration of 1917, the support of the Allies in their aim to create a homeland for the Jewish people in Palestine.

At the same time, the heartland of Jewish life in Eastern Europe went through a profound upheaval. Jewish communities in the old Pale of Settlement had been dislodged, and hundreds of thousands of Jews had been turned into refugees on the war's eastern front. If anything, their situation worsened in 1918, when international war turned into class wars, national independence wars, and civil wars. The centripetal force of the 1914–18 war, its tendency to bring Jews to the center of their states, did not produce lasting benefits for the Jews aside from the Balfour Declaration, and even that event meant little to most of the Jewish masses in Eastern Europe. Of equal importance was that the centrifugal forces of war starved or destabilized much of Eastern Europe and, through the creation of the fantasy of a Judeo-Bolshevik conspiracy, added a toxic element to Central and Eastern European anti-Semitism that helped drive the Nazi movement forward. It is hardly surprising that Jews coined the term the "Drittr Hurban," the Third Catastrophe, for the years 1914–21. The Yiddish phrase put the suffering and destruction of those years alongside the destruction of the Temple of Jerusalem. The Great War was the Third Catastrophe.[28] We know that this destabilization of Jewish life in Eastern Europe was the first tremor before the final earthquake of the Shoah.

It is not possible in this brief essay to do more than say that the Nazis won their war against the Jews in Eastern Europe. During the Second World War, they succeeded in demolishing an entire world. Some of it has been rebuilt, but the complexity, the density, the richness of that world is gone. In effect there has been a shift in the balance of Jewish life in the world. Before the Shoah, roughly 60 percent of the world's Jewish population was in Europe. After 1945, that figure descended to 37 percent. Now Europe is the home for about 10 percent of the world's Jewish population. More Jews live in the New York City metropolitan area today (2022) than in all of Europe.

Two other major changes have marked this profound shift in the center of gravity of Jewish life. During and after the Second World War, and in light of the humanitarian emergency it produced, a shift occurred in many Jewish communities from focusing on synagogue life to targeting communal life.

---

[28] Jay Winter, The Great War and Jewish memory, *Yearbook for European Jewish Literature Studies*, 1 (2014), pp. 13–41.

This emphasis on social service inevitably brought out women's talents and leadership, enabling women to play a larger role in Jewish public life thereafter.

The second change was more subtle and more contested. In the Warsaw ghetto was a remarkable group of Jewish activists who created the "Oneg Shabbat archive." It was a collection of documents about Jewish life left buried underground in large milk containers. Several people were sent out of the ghetto so that after its destruction, someone would retrieve this archive. They did.

The archive has a bit of everything: fashion designs, cookbooks, discussions on the role of women, vignettes of everyday life. It also has a remarkable treatise by a polymath rabbi, Shimon Huberband. He offered a commentary on many Jewish beliefs and practices. Within it is a set of reflections on Jewish martyrdom. The core of his thinking is that martyrdom in Jewish life is a matter of choice, a terrible choice he himself was facing in the Warsaw ghetto; that is where he died a few weeks after writing his treatise. Was martyrdom (in Hebrew *Be'kiddush Hashem*, sanctifying the name of the Lord in death) the only way? Perhaps, Huberband suggested, there was another way, which he called *Be'kiddush HaChayim*, or the sanctification of God by living. His archive was about the mission he never lived to realize.[29]

His work posed a terrible question. Martyrdom, in Jewish life, was a choice. But what choice did infants have? What choice did the more than one million Jewish children have in their fate? What choice did the assimilated Jews in the camps have? Many were people who never identified with Judaism but were sentenced to death anyway. Without a choice, martyrdom lost much of its meaning. Huberband touched a chord: his emphasis on the need to sanctify life was picked up by others, not to make the Shoah any less terrifying, but to help the survivors go beyond it.

There is still much dispute on this matter, but in some respects, we can see that Huberband's legacy is alive and well. References to the term *martyrdom* in books published in Hebrew have declined from the 1940s to the present.[30] If further research supports the view that there has been a shift in Jewish thinking on this subject, then it shows how important a period in Jewish cultural history was the Shoah.

In 1948, the State of Israel was established. This event brought Judaism into line with the problems faced by Christians and Muslims with respect to international politics. We have seen that the politics of the Vatican made it

---

[29] Shimon Huberband, *Kiddush Hashem: Jewish religious and cultural life in Poland during the Shoah* (New York: Yeshiva University Press, 1987), pp. 247ff.

[30] Jay Winter, *War beyond words: Languages of remembrance from the Great War to the present* (Cambridge: Cambridge University Press, 2017), ch. 5.

difficult for even the pope to speak out on moral issues. The moral commitments of the Muslim Brotherhood have been compromised by the violence of radical Islam. Jews too have a moral dilemma. Can they criticize the State of Israel without siding with those who hate Jews? Is anti-Israeli thinking of necessity anti-Semitic? I believe the answer is no, but the question does raise the problem embedded in the cultural history of religion in time of war with which we started this essay. When religion comes into contact with the state in time of war, then the precepts of religion tend to adapt or change.

What of the great Asian religions, Hinduism and Buddhism? Like all other religions, Hinduism is a house of many mansions. It has precepts condemning war at the same time as some Hindus sing praises of warriors. Gurkas fought with distinction in the British army throughout the twentieth century; perhaps one hundred thousand fought in each of the two world wars. Gandhi supported the British cause in 1914 and then promoted nonviolence as a Hindu path to freedom after the war. He was murdered by a Hindu fanatic who was executed for his crime.

Although Buddhism is a religion of nonviolence, a civil war in Sri Lanka between the Buddhist Sinhalese majority and the Hindu Tamil minority took sixty thousand lives over the years 1980 to 2009. States with substantial Buddhist populations have armies today. Witness the case of Myanmar, whose army seized power in 2021. Even before that date, the military acted with particular brutality against the largely Muslim Rohingya people, nearly one million of whom have been driven out of the country and have taken refuge in neighboring Bangladesh. Even with respect to Buddhism, a religion practicing nonviolence as a foundational principle, we find that in some instances, the acid embedded in modern war corrodes or eats through absolutes.

7 Humanitarianism in War

Humanitarian assistance in wartime traditionally was the work of the churches. But in the mid-nineteenth century, a Swiss initiative following the Battle of Solferino in 1859 led to the formation of the Red Cross. Henry Dunant was appalled to see the suffering of wounded soldiers strewn across the battlefield after the fighting had ended. His project, the inspiration for a series of Geneva Conventions that were in place by 1914, was to provide humanitarian assistance during armed conflict to those wounded or sick and no longer capable of fighting on land or at sea. That protection was extended also to prisoners of war.

Humanitarian Work in the Two World Wars

When war broke out in 1914, national Red Cross societies mobilized to assist the medical services of each combatant country. They financed and staffed ambulances, X-ray stations, boats and trains to transport the wounded. They ran hospitals. The Red Cross sent commissions to many theaters other than the Western Front. It was present wherever there was war-related suffering.

The second service the Red Cross provided was equally important. The International Committee of the Red Cross (ICRC), based in Geneva, visited prisoner-of-war camps and inspected the conditions in which prisoners of war lived. It also compiled lists of prisoners and was in a position to compare the names on those lists with the names of soldiers who had gone missing in action. This detective work spanned the globe. Australian families who had no idea if their sons deemed missing in action were alive or dead turned to the Australian Red Cross for help. Cables went from Adelaide to London, from London to Constantinople, and from there to Red Cross agents in the field visiting Turkish prisoner-of-war camps. Missing men were indeed found in this way. Many more were never found.

These Red Cross missions also provided information to families who wanted to know the truth about their sons missing in action. What is most striking about these searches is that they revealed the truth. When a soldier in a hospital or a prisoner-of-war camp was asked about a mate still listed as missing, he frequently replied that he was there when the man was hit. There was no sanitization of the story, no phrases as to how he didn't feel a thing or died in a second. The Red Cross was the conduit for the truth and, by finding it, it offered some families closure. They were perhaps more fortunate than the hundreds of thousands of families who never knew what had happened to their loved ones.

At the end of the war, the League of Red Cross Societies was founded by Britain, France, Italy, Japan and the United States. Its aim was to extend the mission of the Red Cross beyond war to peacetime disasters and emergencies. The International Committee of the Red Cross saw this interloper as a competitor and as a thoroughly American attempt to take over the direction of humanitarian work. The League was not universal; it had the right to keep out the Red Cross societies of the defeated Central Powers.

The two organizations found a way, though, to work side by side. That was inevitable because of the power of American cash and clout in international affairs. From 1915, Herbert Hoover had led a private American effort to feed the children of occupied Belgium and France. At the end of the war, Hoover's food aid program became much bigger and official in character.

Figure 13 Herbert Hoover and Polish children in Warsaw, 1920.
Source: Bettmann via Getty Images

The American Relief Administration (ARA), a US-government-sponsored organization, fed more than a million malnourished German children, the youth of America's former enemy, after the war. The ARA also offered food and other essential supplies to populations from Finland to Turkey, including Russia, then in the midst of a brutal civil war. In Figure 13, we see Hoover with a group of admiring Polish children in Warsaw in 1920.

The twilight zone between war and peace in 1918–23 also brought another important player into the field of humanitarian aid. That was the League of Nations. Through the efforts of an extraordinary Arctic explorer, scientist, and Norwegian patriot, Fridtjof Nansen, the League found a way to repatriate prisoners of war held long after 1918 from Russia to Germany. Nansen provided papers named Nansen passports to Russian people stripped of their nationality by the new Bolshevik regime. And, as the League of Nations High Commissioner for Refugees, he found a way to use the League's resources to fight endemic and epidemic diseases, rife among refugees, and to find a solution to the problems faced by nearly one million Greek Orthodox residents of Turkey who had fled the fighting in the Greek-Turkish war of 1919–23. That solution was a compulsory population exchange whereby space would be found in Greece for the refugees from Turkey by expelling all Muslims residing in Greece, except in western Thrace. Nansen's belief was that "unmixing" populations would enable both groups to start their lives again in their new homes.

Neither the Red Cross nor the League of Nations found a solution to the problem of more than one million survivors of the Armenian genocide of 1915. Helping them survive in makeshift refugee camps in Syria and Lebanon was Near East Relief. It came into existence in 1915 as the American Committee on Armenian Atrocities and over more than a decade provided essential aid for the survivors of genocide. The League of Nations was a major player in this effort as well, giving it a more secular and transnational character. Prior to 1914, the Protestant voluntary traditions and Christian missionaries had propelled humanitarian work forward. After 1918, humanitarian work was transnational and nondenominational. Thus began the transition from humanitarian work as part of what was known condescendingly in the West as the "civilizing mission" to a new kind of philanthropy, resting not on Christianity but on ideas about universal rights. In this new configuration, women played a particularly important role.[31]

The coming to power of the Nazi Party in Germany in 1933 marked the beginning of a new phase in the history of humanitarian relief. After a few cautious months of tiptoeing around the League of Nations commitment to protect minority rights, in particular in Silesia, Germany withdrew from the organization and intensified its persecution of Jews. Between 1933 and 1939, approximately four hundred thousand Jews left Germany and Austria. Finding refuge for these emigrés was almost always difficult, occasionally impossible. The Dutch accepted Jewish refugees only temporarily; they could come in transit. Canada's doors were virtually closed in the 1930s. Entry to the United States was strictly limited. One passenger liner, the S.S. *St. Louis*, was refused entry to the United States and Cuba in 1939 and returned to Europe; approximately one-third of those passengers were killed in the Shoah. South American countries were more amenable to accepting refugees, especially highly skilled people like doctors. But in most cases, refugees needed financial help to survive.

Jewish philanthropic organizations, themselves still recovering from the Great Depression, provided essential support. At the heart of their work was

---

[31] See Davide Rodogno, *Night on earth: A history of international humanitarianism in the Near East, 1918–1930* (Cambridge: Cambridge University Press, 2021), and Keith David Watenpaugh, The League of Nations' rescue of Armenian genocide survivors and the making of modern humanitarianism, 1920–1927, *American Historical Review*, 115, 5 (December 2010), pp. 1315–39.

Figure 14 German Jewish children en route to Switzerland through the
Kindertransport, 1939.
Source: Imagno/Contributor via Getty Images

the Jewish Joint Distribution Committee, set up in 1914 to help Jews survive the economic crisis of the outbreak of war in the Ottoman empire. American Jewry's financial aid was mobilized by both Zionist and non-Zionist organizations. Coordinating efforts in Britain was the Central Jewish Fund for German Jewish Relief, which sent agents to interview refugees. One such agent, stockbroker Julian Layton, dealt with Adolph Eichmann in expediting Jewish emigration. That was his job before the outbreak of the war in 1939.

Bringing children out of Germany, Austria, and Czechoslovakia was the target of particular humanitarian groups. After the nationwide pogrom of November 9–10, 1938 in Germany, British Home Secretary Sir Samuel Hoare agreed to take groups of refugees into Britain, but only temporarily. The Refugee Children's Movement helped find the funds for travel to Britain, a £50 voucher for reemigration, and foster homes for ten thousand children. In Figure 14, we see German Jewish children en route to Switzerland and safety through the *Kindertransport* in 1939. The last train taking children out of Germany left on September 1, 1939, the day Germany invaded Poland. Another British humanitarian, Nicholas Winton, like Layton a stockbroker, got 669 Jewish children out of Prague before the gates closed.

Once war was declared, German refugees to Britain and other Allied countries became enemy aliens. This new status led to questions as to whether the Nazis had hidden spies among the refugees. Approximately seventy thousand German men went before internment tribunals, which found that the vast majority were victims of Nazi persecution and posed no security threat. Then the disaster in France and at Dunkirk in May 1940 changed everything. Churchill, following the advice of his Joint Chiefs of Staff, approved the mass internment of German and Italian male aliens. Overcrowding in camps in England led to the shipping of seven thousand such men to internment camps in Canada and Australia. One of the boats taking them to Canada was sunk en route with the loss of seven hundred lives.

The internment of enemy aliens had happened before, between 1914 and 1918. Both then and during 1939–40, internment showed in stark terms the limits of the humanitarian project. In May 1940, probably the worst month in British military history, fears of a German invasion meant that state security came before everything else. This was the rule all over the world. The French interned refugees from Spain in 1939 and from Germany in 1940. The internment of approximately one hundred and twenty thousand Japanese-Americans by the US government pointed in the same direction.

During the Second World War, humanitarian work continued along the lines set out during the First. One difference was that the ICRC's stated policy of working with recognized states meant that the inspection of German concentration camps wound up serving German propaganda purposes. In the Theresienstadt camp in Czechoslovakia, the German authorities organized a huge charade to persuade gullible Swiss agents of the ICRC that the inmates were well treated. It took decades for the ICRC to outlive this massive error.

The American Jewish Joint Distribution Committee helped in a host of ways, most undercover, to spirit out of Nazi-occupied Europe approximately eighty thousand Jewish people. The Joint (as it was known) found a way to get money to Jewish groups, including those planning the Warsaw ghetto revolt in 1943. It also provided essential support for roughly twenty thousand German and Austrian Jews who had found a safe haven in Shanghai.

The fate of one group there shows how complex and multifaceted was the humanitarian world during the war. Members of one of the great rabbinical academies of Europe, the Mir Yeshiva, left Belorussia for the Polish city of Vilna at the outbreak of the Second World War. They desperately sought to get out of Europe and their lives were saved through diplomatic humanitarianism. A Dutch consul in Vilna offered the entire yeshiva visas to the Caribbean island of Curaçao. The problem remained that they could not go west during the war. The only way to freedom was to go east. A Japanese vice-consul, Chiume

Sugihara, provided everyone with a visa to enter Japan. Traveling across Siberia with Soviet travel visas, they got to Japan and then to Shanghai. There, through financial support from donors all over the world, including the Joint, they survived the war.

Postwar

The most important aspect of humanitarian history in the postwar years was the passage of the Fourth Geneva Convention in 1949. It established rules of protection for civilians in wartime and in occupied territories. This advance was a clear recognition of the civilianization of war and of Nazi crimes. In common article 3, the 1949 Convention also met the urgent need to extend protection to those suffering from subnational or transnational armed conflicts. Humanitarian action operated in this new framework from that point on.

Initially, after the end of the war, the problem of displaced persons in Europe and Asia was immense. The Nazis had rendered much of Europe's Jewish population stateless, and most survivors had no interest in going back to the scene of the crime. Most wanted to emigrate to the United States but could not do so due to American immigration restrictions. Under these circumstances, groups of former concentration camp prisoners formed their own self-help organizations. Recovering their health and dignity, they insisted on the right to choose their own destinations and futures. Zionist groups helped a substantial number emigrate to Palestine, but there too restrictions on entry by the British Mandatory powers posed problems.

Other population movements were unfolding at the same time. Perhaps fourteen million ethnic Germans who lived in areas conquered by the Nazis or in those occupied by Soviet forces were uprooted and fled west. Their assimilation into West German society was a remarkable achievement and an essential part of the construction of the new democratic Germany.

The pacification by 1950 of a Europe now divided into two armed camps shifted the focus of humanitarian work elsewhere. The end of the Mandatory system the UN had inherited from the League of Nations produced explosions of violence in the Middle East. Among those who suffered the most from war in the late 1940s were the Palestinians.

The UN provided the framework within which many of the first efforts on behalf of civilian victims of wars were helped. The UN Relief and Rehabilitation Agency, which worked from 1943 to 1947, set an example others followed thereafter. Among the most long-lasting is the UN Relief and Works Agency for Palestinian refugees in the Middle East. Established in 1949, it is still in operation. Shorter lived was the UN Korea Reconstruction Agency (1950–3). More than two hundred nongovernmental organizations (NGOs) were established in the early years of the UN. They set a pattern of NGO-led initiatives still evident today.

Food aid and foreign aid overlapped with humanitarian aid to civilians affected by war. But humanitarian aid for war victims inevitably became caught up in Cold War politics. Stalin turned down Marshall Plan aid, and Communist China was off limits to American aid in the 1950s and after. Catholic food aid in Vietnam was restricted to the US-led South Vietnamese forces.

There were continuities with earlier periods. The Red Cross was there to provide assistance, for example in Kashmir during the terrible period of violence following the partition of India in 1947. Fifteen years later, Western NGOs, in particular Oxfam and CARE, acted to save lives in war-torn Biafra in the late 1960s. Out of this conflict was born one long-lasting NGO, Médecins sans frontières, still in operation today. A new era of NGO-led campaigns on behalf of the victims of war started here.

In the years that have followed, both the UN and the still-growing NGO world have acted to bring relief to the victims of war, mostly in the global south. The end of the Cold War did not see a subsidence of armed conflicts but their multiplication. The UN became directly involved in internecine conflicts in Iraq, Somalia and the former Yugoslavia. But of perhaps greater significance was the failure of the UN to act to stop genocide in Rwanda in 1994. That failure reinforced the emergence of the doctrine of the responsibility to protect, mobilized by the North Atlantic Treaty Organization (NATO) in response to Serbian attacks in Kosovo. It also provided the political support for the establishment of the International Criminal Court in 2002 and its judicial arraignment of those accused of war crimes, crimes against humanity, and genocide.

The judicial framework that has emerged over the past twenty years has given humanitarian movements new instruments with which to protect those injured in war. Older approaches are still needed; witness the refugee tragedies accompanying the civil war in Syria today (2022). But the essence of humanitarian work has changed over time. International law makes a difference. What brought the new regime about was a nearly universal sense that material aid, while essential, was not enough. The braiding together of humanitarian rights with human rights in international tribunals has provided a roof over the heads of those endangered by war. It is a thin cover for them, but a cover nevertheless, one that shows how much our common understanding of war and our ideas about how to limit its horrors have changed over the past century.

8 The Visual Arts

The Visual Arts in War

Throughout the twentieth century, states have placed the visual arts at the core of their propaganda efforts in wartime. Poster artists were commissioned by every combatant country to illustrate the cause, in particular to persuade civilians to help finance the war effort through war loans. The subjects these posters treated were conventional icons of heroism chosen to glorify the nation and demonize its enemy. If we are fighting against monsters, these artists affirmed, then there is no room for doubt. Patriotic images occluded pacifist messages everywhere.

Iconic images of national identity and ancient rivalries were readily available from many sources. Among them were the so-called *Images d'Epinal*, stylized and childlike posters made popular in the 1830s throughout Europe as part of the cult of Napoleon. Naive art of many kinds brought out the supposedly eternal and sacred characteristics of peoples. Religious icons in the Orthodox world served this purpose well. The proliferation of this kind of ethnic propaganda included works by modern artists attached to ancient or rural motifs. In Russia, Kandinsky, Chagall, and Goncharova explored folk art in wartime, as did Raoul Dufy in France. This return to traditional motifs and images marked cultural life after 1914.

The First World War generated a mixture of initiatives from the ancient to the completely modern. The Allies were quicker off the mark than were the Central Powers to see the propaganda potential of the cinema. Partly this was a reflection of the autocratic nature of the German and Austro-Hungarian empires, but it showed too the degree to which the Allies recognized the significance of the consent of the governed in the waging of industrial war. The most important propaganda figure of the war was the Londoner turned Hollywood star Charlie Chaplin. He starred not only on the silver screen but also in war rallies to raise money for the war effort in the United States. In Figure 15, we see Chaplin signing his comic masterpiece *Shoulder Arms*, released in 1918. German officials woke up to the uses of the cinema only in the last year of the war, providing subventions for the Universum-Film Aktiengesellschaft (UFA), founded in December 1917.[32]

All combatants also employed painters and graphic artists to document the gigantic effort each country was waging for victory. Official art had boundaries. It could not portray the bloody carnage of battle, but it concentrated on the epic

---

[32] Rainer Rother (ed.), *Die UFA 1917–1945. Das deutsche Bildimperium* (Berlin: Deutsches Historisches Museum, Berlin, 1992).

Figure 15 Charlie Chaplin in *Shoulder Arms*, 1918.
Source: Photo by LMPC via Getty Images

dimensions of the conflict. When war artists showed the dead, their work was censored. The work of the British war artist Christopher Nevinson, entitled ironically *Paths of Glory*, was censored. Nevinson showed them anyway in an exhibition in London in March 1918, but with a brown paper strip covering the dead. On the strip was the word "Censored." Other war artists were more content to stay within the conventional guidelines of how to use painting to support the war effort.

Publishing caricatures of the dead bodies of grotesque and terrifying enemies was entirely acceptable. Only in France did the censor lift the injunction against showing "our" war dead. Since the whole of the north of France was occupied by millions of German troops, the sight of dead French soldiers caused little alarm or surprise in France. The civilian populations of Germany and Britain were not allowed to see similar images in the press.[33]

The 1914–18 war was the moment when photography went to war. The marketing of the Kodak vest pocket camera, not much bigger than today's

---

[33] Joëlle Beurier, *Photographier la Grande Guerre: France Allemagne: L'héroisme et la violence dans les magazines* (Rennes: Presses universitaires de Rennes, 2016).

iPhone, to soldiers ensured that military authorities could not prevent images of the battlefield and of combat circulating freely among soldiers and their families. Soldiers put together photo albums by the thousands to show their children and grandchildren their war and the exotic places they had visited. This evidence demolishes the older notion that civilians have no idea what war is like. They saw what the soldiers saw and what the soldiers sent home to them.

Visual propaganda of all kinds attended the wars that broke out after the Armistice of 1918 as well. It was all too easy to switch the captions but not the monstrous images of wartime posters and postcards to fit the new and vile enemies whose defeat was coming. What made the visual culture of hatred even worse was the Russian Revolution of 1917. Image of class conflict merged with nationalist struggles to create postwar propaganda as vulgar and oversimplified as that which had preceded it. By the early 1920s, a new element was added to the witches' brew of hatred in visual form. Anti-Semitic caricature joined the visual repertoire of the anticommunist right. Images of that absurd and yet easily marketed menace to civilization, the Judeo-Bolshevik conspiracy, enabled the newly formed National Socialist Party in Germany and its epigone to disseminate racial stereotypes with ease.

By the 1930s, it was evident to everyone that 1914–18 was not the war to end all wars. In 1937, in the midst of armed conflict in Spain and China, all the great powers and many smaller ones created national pavilions for the Paris International Exhibition of the Arts and Techniques of Modern Life. It was a celebration of enlightenment and science. Underground barges on the Seine surfaced at night to illuminate Paris, the City of Light. It was one hundred years since the birth of the railway and three hundred years since the publication of Descartes's *Discours sur la méthode*. The march of science and technology was the leitmotif of the expo.

Cinema was the art of the new electric age. The socialists who ran the French government and hosted the expo pulled out all the stops in welcoming Leni Riefenstahl, Hitler's favorite filmmaker. In their pavilions, the great powers highlighted not their weaponry but their artistry and ingenuity in applying science to everyday life. But there was a counterpoint so powerful that it has eclipsed virtually everything that happened in the expo.

I am referring to the installation in the pavilion of the Spanish Republic of Picasso's painting *Guernica*. It is probably the most important work of art about war in the twentieth century. In the center of the painting is a light bulb. It announces the use of electricity to arm bombers to kill civilians below in the Basque capital city of Guernica. So much for the utopia of science transforming the world, a theme developed in the same exhibition by French painter Raoul Dufy.

Figure 16 Picasso's *Guernica*, 1937, now in the Reina Sofia Museum, Madrid.
Source: Photo by Denis Doyle/Getty Images

Picasso's *Guernica* was done at warp speed in the two weeks after he saw a newsreel about the destruction of the center of Guernica by the German Condor Legion on April 26, 1937. It shows those already dead and those about to die under the bombs still to fall. There is no better image bringing home the horror of the civilianization of war than Picasso's masterpiece. In Figure 16, we see his *Guernica* in its current home in the Reina Sofia Museum in Madrid.

In the Second World War, all the visual arts were deployed by the combatant countries in the support of the morale of both soldiers and civilians. One unusual development in Britain was the efflorescence of religious art in a war configured as being waged by the Allies in the defense of Christianity. The greatest war memorial in Britain built in the postwar years was Sir Basil Spence's architectural masterpiece, Coventry Cathedral. The ruined shell of the old cathedral was left as it was after German bombing on November 14–15, 1940. At right angles to it, the new cathedral stands. As we see in Figure 17, at the end of the nave is the largest tapestry ever woven, Graham Sutherland's *Christ in Glory in the Tetramorph*.

For the church's consecration in 1962, Benjamin Britten conducted his "War Requiem," braiding together the poetry of the First World War with the discordant sounds of the air war in the Second. At that event, we see the last moment that the imagery of war was configured in specifically Christian terms.

Figure 17 Graham Sutherland's tapestry *Christ in Glory in the Tetramorph* in
Coventry Cathedral, 1962.
Source: Photo by Mike Kemp/In Pictures via Getty Images

Thereafter, secular images of war like Picasso's predominated in many parts of
the world.

The cinema was one area in which the sacred and the secular were still mixed
together in the visual arts. One extraordinary example is the pacifist film *The
Burmese Harp* by the Japanese filmmaker Kon Ishikawa. The film was released
in 1956 in black and white and reappeared in a color version in 1985. It tells the
story of a Japanese soldier who at the end of the war is given a mission to
convince some comrades still holding out in the mountains of Burma that it is
futile to carry on fighting. He fails in that mission and, on the way back to his
unit, he passes the unburied remains of many Japanese soldiers. The traumatic
shock of seeing vultures tearing these bodies apart stops him in his tracks. He
starts burying the bodies around him and takes shelter in a Buddhist monastery.
He becomes a monk and stays in Burma despite the pleas of his comrades to
return home. In Figure 18, we see Soji Yasui as Mizushima holding the Burmese
harp he learns to play in Kon Ichikawa's film.

This film is remarkable on many levels, but for our purposes what it shows is
that war films came in many different forms. In the post-1945 period, there were
two kinds of war films. The first may be termed realistic in that they tried with
special effects to persuade viewers that they can see war as it is. The second
form is indirect in that it never let viewers believe that they are seeing war as it

THE BURMESE HARP

Figure 18 Soji Yasui in Kon Ichikawa's *The Burmese Harp*, 1956.
Source: Photo by Brandon Films/Getty Images

is. Another way to make this contrast is to speak of films that aim at showing spectacle and others that aim at showing tragedy. The greatest war films are in the latter category.[34]

Since the Second World War, the cinema industry has provided hundreds of films about war. Each country's film archive has different emphases and conventions. By and large, films showing war as spectacle far outnumber those showing war as tragedy, but the defeat in Vietnam, together with the uncertain outcome of the wars in Iraq and Afghanistan, have given war films a more somber tone in recent years. Equally striking is the portrayal of the soldier's fragility more than his ferocity. In the early twenty-first century, there is a more nuanced portrayal of war and of soldiers as victims of war in cinema than there was during and after the Second World War.

---

[34] Winter, *War beyond words*, pp.75–6.

Part of the reason for this change in cinematic treatments of war is that the Shoah has become a central element in the history of the Second World War. Films about the Nazi genocide against the Jews have shifted attention away from the heroism of military combat to the heroism of civilian survival. Similarly installation artists like Anselm Kiefer have used kabbalistic myths as sources for indirect representations of the Holocaust. His seminal work *The Smashing of the Vessels* is a meditation on theodicy, the question of how, if God is all good, evil got into the world. Using lead sheets to suggest burned books and broken glass to evoke the pogrom of November 9–10, 1938, in Germany, Kiefer created a visual memorial to the Holocaust of lasting significance.

The Effect of War on the Visual Arts

It is easier to describe the image of war in the visual arts over the past century than it is to say in what ways war has affected the development of the visual arts. The long-term move away from realism and toward abstraction started well before the 1914–18 war and continued throughout much of the twentieth century. Similarly, innovations in conceptual art, pop art, or digital art have multiple sources only superficially connected to the violence of the twentieth century.

Nevertheless, we can refer to a number of areas in which the upheaval of the two world wars affected the nature of the visual arts. The first is through the destruction of transnational networks. One of the most fertile periods of art were the years before 1914. Artists from many different countries shared a common interest in creating a revolutionary art for a globalizing world. One publication aiming at showcasing this remarkable moment in art was *Blaue Reiter*, produced in Munich by German and Russian artists. It was supposed to be an annual review but ceased publication after one issue. August 1914 put an end to it.

All over the world, the nation became the unit of artistic creativity. The art of the Allies could be celebrated, to be sure, but art turned inward when war was declared. Artists had a hard time in war. There was a shortage in paper, canvas, and paint. And the art market, robustly international in 1914, shrank in the first three years of the war. With American entry into the war in 1917, those with deep pockets returned to Paris and fueled a major expansion of the art market over the period 1917–19.

Second, in some parts of Europe occurred what the artist Jean Cocteau called a return to order. By that he meant that after 1914, figuration returned to painting after having been eclipsed for some time by abstraction. Picasso and Braque moved away from cubism for a time. Picasso entered what some call a neoclassical phase, and Braque focused on still-life art. Were these moves a reaction to the shattering of so many bodies during the war?

Perhaps more directly related to the war was, in some circles, the eclipse of the admiration for Italian futurism with its worship of machines and speed. No one needed reminding that machines crushed men, though here too there were different responses in different parts of the world. Following the Russian Revolution, a new form of creative art called constructivism sought to turn the artist into a mechanic or engineer with tools in his hands.

In Germany, the Bauhaus school aimed at breaking down the wall separating artists and artisans. It established a system of education replicating the medieval guild system, with masters and apprentices replacing professors and students. Those accepted to work in the Bauhaus were paid and went on to important careers in architecture, design, painting, and sculpture. The Bauhaus was left-wing in outlook and did not survive the Nazi accession to power in the 1930s.

The term *surrealism* was invented in 1916 by the French poet of Polish origin Guillaume Apollinaire, but it took off as an artistic movement after the end of the war. He died in 1918 before seeing its heyday, but shared the view that realism was an empty vessel incapable of interpreting the violent events of the day. An antiwar movement, Dada, the name of which derived from an infant's nonsense words, emerged during the war and stimulated many to go beyond reason in their art. To these artists, if the rational had led to the worst war in history, then the surreal was the only place to go after 1918. Uniting the conscious and unconscious realms led to explorations in dreamworlds like those found in the work of the Spanish painter Salvador Dali.

After the Second World War, abstract expressionist artists, mostly but not exclusively based in New York, continued to explore the terrain opened up by surrealism. So did Francis Bacon in Britain. The German artist Joseph Beuys, severely wounded on the Eastern Front in the Second World War, went on to become a professor of monumental sculpture in Düsseldorf. He was dismissed during the turbulent years following 1968 but retained his belief that the artist could act as a kind of shaman linking art to the world of spirits. In some respects, Beuys and Anselm Kiefer, who worked with him in Düsseldorf, pointed back to the world of *Blaue Reiter* and to its pre-1914 search for a way to braid together science and spirituality in art.

War Museums

A final area of work that shows the linkage between war and the visual arts is the construction of war museums in many countries in all parts of the world. Staring in 1914, these museum projects aimed at preserving a record of the gigantic upheaval of war. In this effort, governments provided the cash, and in many cases, former soldiers and politicians provided the political support needed to see these massive projects through to completion.

War museums emerged in most combatant countries in the twenty years following the First World War. The leader in the field for a considerable period of time was the Imperial War Museum. Founded in 1917, it moved to its current site in 1936. It occupies the grounds of the old "Bedlam" insane asylum on the south bank of the Thames. Its transnational approach differed from similar ventures in France, Germany, and elsewhere. The Australian War Memorial, for example, became a national shrine after its opening in 1941. It is located along a monumental visual axis now including many war memorials to particular wars. In the distance is the new national parliament in Canberra. The layout suggests that politicians need to bear in mind at all times the sacrifices made for freedom. "Taps" is played every evening at the Australian War Memorial in honor of the men who died in uniform.

War museums came to the communist world after 1945. In Russia as well as in its satellites, the story of the hard-won victory in the Great Patriotic War occluded any mention of the First World War, in which two million Russian soldiers had died. History started with communism, the founders of these museums believed, and therefore museums focused on the war the communists waged and they believed (with some justification) won from 1941 to 1945.

The emergence of war museums in Asia and Africa has a different trajectory, one related to the struggle for independence from colonial rule. The Swatantra Sangram Sangrahalaya, opened in 1994 in Delhi, is a museum dedicated to documenting India's struggle to break away from British rule. The military Museum of the Chinese People's Revolution was completed in 1960. In recent years, local museums have opened in many parts of China. There the story of the Nationalists has appeared alongside that of the Communists in the war against Japan. Such museums reflect the foreign policy interests of the government.[35]

In every one of these museums, designers faced the problem as to how to represent war. Most use heroic conventions to do so. One important exception is Ernst Friedrich's Anti-war Museum. It opened in Berlin in 1925 and was destroyed by storm troopers in 1933. This was no surprise given Friedrich's use of photography to present relentlessly the horrors of war. In recent years, though, other museums have taken on an antiwar attitude, though one that stops short of Friedrich's polemic. Among them are the Military Museum in Dresden and the Historial de la Grande Guerre in Péronne, France. Given the need for state funding in most cases, it is likely that most museums will continue to

---

[35] Mitter, *China's good war.*

present positive images of a nation's soldiers alongside a negative image of the devastation war brings in its wake, though the field is wide open for innovation, in particular on the transnational level.

9 Prose, Poetry, and the Voice of the Witness

War Poetry

One of the most striking developments in the cultural history of the First World War is the emergence of poetic forms that break with romantic tropes about war. This phenomenon began in Britain, but over the past century, it has appeared in many languages. What Wilfred Owen called "the pity of war, the pity war distills" found expression everywhere.

The cadences of poetry in different languages were distinctive and the archive from which poets drew in Urdu or Chinese was not the same as those in Greek and Turkish. In the short space available here, we cannot do justice to the efflorescence of poetic expression all over the world. What we can do is speak of a new category in poetic discourse that emerged in 1914 and still exists today. That category is the work of soldier-poets, a composite noun separating these authors from those who wrote as observers either close to or remote from the front lines. The subject position of the writer matters, since to write from within the belly of the whale, as it were, is radically different from writing about the belly of the whale from an outsider's perspective.

The mass mobilization of the First World War created this new category of war poets. In the first week of the war alone, hundreds of thousands of poems appeared in the press of all the major combatants. Most of it is what we term doggerel or pedestrian verse. Almost of all of it was uplifting and romantic in character. And how could it have been otherwise? These versifiers were ignorant of industrial war, even though the effects of artillery on the human body were not a secret. The Balkan wars of 1912 and 1913 had provided abundant photographic evidence of what a shell does to the human body. But that was not the picture most people shared. Instead they conjured up images of gallant cavalry charges and sweeping troop movements.

That war of movement came to a crushing end in a couple of months. By the end of 1914, a new kind of war, industrialized siege warfare, emerged, and it was against the backdrop of this mutation in armed conflict that war poetry was born. What was new was that the scale of war changed to such a degree that the power of killing machines dwarfed the ability of men to protect themselves. The battle of artillery against the human body was so lopsided that the only way men could stay alive was by descending deep under the earth. The trench system that emerged from 1915 on was a troglodyte world, one in which the rhythms of nature and birdsong were but distant memories. A blasted landscape filled with the detritus of war was far from the bucolic countryside of nineteenth-century poetry.

There were romantic poets who continued to write rhapsodies about the glory of war. Similarly, propagandists used language in such a way as to separate it from the world the soldiers saw. Soldier-poets wrote against the degeneration of language in verse and prose. Part of their purpose was to scrub down what the American critic Edmund Wilson called patriotic gore to get to the essence of language as a carrier of truth, not lies or gross distortions of reality.[36]

War poets wrote adversary verse, not against the enemy, but against the lies both sides told about the nobility of war. The force of their verse came out of the tension embedded in the subject position of soldier-poets. As poets, they used language to affirm humane values. As soldiers, they destroyed human bodies and saw cruelties that could not be justified under any system of values. War poetry is therefore rooted in a contradiction in terms, and out of that violent opposition, poets spoke to the world about the new kind of war born in 1914. There were many different ways poets went about their work. Here I will discuss only four. The first is the destruction of sentimentality. Soldier-poets in many countries waged war against the maudlin, the cheap, and the completely ignorant phrases that poured out of the popular press and official communiqués about war. The British officer Siegfried Sassoon wrote this verse in 1918 about what we now call the kitsch of popular entertainment in wartime:

> I'd like to see a Tank come down the stalls,
> Lurching to rag-time tunes, or "Home, sweet Home,"
> And there'd be no more jokes in Music-halls To mock the riddled
>   corpses round Bapaume.

The title of the poem is "Blighters," derived from an Indian word for home, or "Blighty." Those who sang cheery songs about war drew out his rage.

A second strategy of denunciation of heroic language is the presentation of a soldier's death as a banal event. In Figure 19, we see the Israeli poet Yehuda Amichai. He fought in the 1948 war and cut down the sight of a fellow soldier's death to its bare bones, as it were. In "Lamentations on the War Dead," he wrote about his friend "Dikki":

---

[36] The phrase is from Edmond Wilson, *Patriotic gore: Studies in the literature of the American Civil War* (New York: W. W. Norton, 1962).

Figure 19 Yehuda Amichai, Israeli poet.

Dikki was hit
Like the watertower in Yad Mordechay. Hit. A hole in the belly.
  Everything Streamed out of him.
But he remained standing like that In the landscape of my memory,
Like the watertower in Yad Mordechay. Not far from there, he fell
A bit northward, near Chulekat.

Amichai was a master of a third poetic strategy, that of outright denunciation. Here the poet demolishes the theologians and true believers who shout that God is on their side. They were there in 1914; they are there today. He was not a practicing Jew but knew the Bible well. In his poem "God Pities the Kindergarten Children," he wrote:

God pities the kindergarten children He pities the schoolchildren less
And He does not pity the adults at all. He leaves them alone
And sometimes they are forced to crawl on all fours
In the burning sand,
To get to the first-aid station And they are bleeding

Here are echoes of the poem Wilfred Owen wrote in 1918 about the story of Abraham's sacrifice of Isaac, stopped in the Bible by an angel at the very last minute. Not in Owen's verse, "The Parable of the Old Man and the Young." Abraham doesn't hear the message to spare his son: "But the old man would not so, but *slew* his *son*. And half the seed of *Europe, one by one.*"

A fourth war poet's strategy is to suggest that war is beyond language and that perhaps only silence can capture its horrors. Walter McDonald was a US Air Force pilot who served in Vietnam. In "Rocket Attack," he reflects on his daughter back home, playing with ducks in a pond, worlds away from the Pacific Ocean and the war in Vietnam. The poet prays she never knows what her father knows, that she never hears or sees war.

> Daughter, oh God, my daughter may she never
> safe at home
> Never hear the horrible
> sucking sound a rocket makes when it

Cutting off the verse before the last verb, McDonald leaves us alone to imagine carnage in silence, and to imagine the silence of the men like McDonald who brought the wounded and the dead back with him, inside his mind and heart, when he came home. Silence is a language of poetic memory.

War Books

The cultural critic Paul Fussell explored the world of war poetry and prose through the powerful interpretative lenses provided by the Canadian literary scholar Northrop Frye. He suggested that all narratives adopted one of three different strategies. The first is to tell the story as a myth through the eyes of a hero whose freedom of action, like that of Achilles, is much greater than ours, approaching that of the gods. The second is to tell the story in a realistic mode, through the eyes of a hero just like us, with our limitations and foibles. We look at them as we look in a mirror, as we see the characters in a Dickens novel. The third is to use an ironic mode, in which the hero's freedom is less than ours and we have a sense that we are looking at a world of "bondage, frustration, or absurdity."[37] Here we are in the world of Franz Kafka or Samuel Beckett.

Fussell posits that First World War poetry and prose started at the mythic level, moved into the realistic, and then focused on the ironic, while circling back in a way to the mythic. Irony means to say one thing and mean another. The ironic mode is to adopt shifting moral positions, as befitted the situation of

---

[37] Paul Fussell, *The Great War and modern memory* (Oxford: Oxford University Press, 1975), p. 337.

soldier poets and novelists. Are these writers prowar or antiwar? The answer is both, but in different ways at different times. Do war writers tell the truth? Yes, but at times, they recount incidents that could not have happened but are true. That is, they are so beyond our prewar sense experience that they appear fantastic, nightmarish, out of this world. And as an American soldier-writer who served in Vietnam, Tim O'Brien put it, if someone presents an event in war as true, don't believe him or her. The word "truth" shimmers in the violence of war and then falls apart. What we come to see is that there are truths about war, but not one inviolable truth. Here is irony in action: destroying the authority of truth in a war story is the only way to preserve the truth about war.

The variety and richness of fiction and memoirs written by soldiers who saw combat in the twentieth century is truly dazzling. The reason to raise the critical positions developed by Frye and Fussell is not to suggest that they describe all writing by soldiers or ex-soldiers. It is to provide a critical point of departure to show how different are the works of African, Asian, and Latin American soldier-writers when compared to those of their North American or European counterparts.

In addition, the boundary between soldier-writers and those who accompanied soldiers at the front – journalists, nurses, priests, auxiliaries, prostitutes, political operatives, and spies – has always been porous. Fussell had an essentialist view of soldiers-writers. That is, he believed that their direct experience brought them insights others could not have. I do not subscribe to this position, which is contradicted by literary talent. Ernest Hemingway was not at Caporetto in 1917, and even when he got to the Italian front, he reported on it as a journalist and not as a soldier. And yet his novel *Farewell to Arms* (1929) is one of the great war novels. The French writer Céline wrote a great war novel, *Journey to the End of the Night* (1932), but his military service was limited to being shot in the arm in the first months of the war. He pretended he had shell shock and showed as proof a photograph of himself with a head bandage. That cloth was there because of toothache. He knew nothing of the war in the trenches and everything about human degradation and depravity. Was he a soldier-writer? Yes and no. The category must be treated with caution.

Finally, in the past, the category of soldier-writer has left out many women writers who were at the front. They had the right to speak because they were there, under bombardment, on troop ships, in hospitals. And they had contact with male bodies, in particular as nurses. Nevertheless, their voices have been marginalized. When we speak of soldier-poets or soldier-writers, we speak of categories that emerged at a time when women's writing was excluded from what we call the canon, the accepted body of literature on war. To paraphrase Virginia Woolf, in the mansion of soldiers' writing, women writers had no rooms of their own. That omission cannot be justified; rectifying it is one of the challenges of scholarship in the coming years.

The Witness: Beyond Silence

There is a third category of testimony about war that has become more and more central to the cultural history of war over the past fifty years. Avishai Margalit was the first to speak of the category of moral witnesses. Like soldier-poets, this term is a compound noun, inseparable into its two parts. Moral witnesses are victims of the violence and cruelties of war who know its ugliness from within and who live to tell later generations what happened to them. They are insiders. They bear on their bodies and in their minds the scars of ill treatment, prejudice, and hatred. They are not journalists or historians who approach the subject of suffering from outside, but people who have lived the stories they are prepared to tell.

One facet of the moral witness parallels that of the soldier-poets and prose writers. It is the anger of their voices, not only against the perpetrators, but also against those who sanitize the past, who tell uplifting and noble stories about situations where such actions either never happened at all or never happened in the way these "immorally" uplifting witnesses pretend they did.

One small incident may stand for the larger problem raised by moral and immoral witnesses. Leon Welizcker Wells was a Jewish inmate of the Janowska concentration camp outside Lviv in today's Ukraine. He was a *Sondercommando* charged with cleaning up the site of extermination. When he read Hassidic tales of the heroism and miracles surrounding the pious inmates of the same camp, he was irate. How dare they sanctify hell? Wells took it as his task to strip away from accounts of the Shoah any redeeming features at all.[38]

Of even greater importance than sanitization of the story of the Shoah is what is called Holocaust denial. War crimes trials in the aftermath of the Second World War created a documentary record of these atrocities. Leon Welizcker Wells was a witness both at Nuremberg and at the Eichmann trial in Jerusalem. And yet, despite these two trials, a small number of people remained who still cast doubt on whether the Shoah actually took place. The proliferation over the past forty years of archives filled with the testimony of survivors of the Shoah makes it almost impossible for anyone to believe the deniers.

---

[38] Jay Winter, *Remembering war: The Great War between history and memory* (New Haven, CT: Yale University Press, 2007), p. 253–60. Wells told me about himself and his mission to correct the record in the Fortunoff in the Fortunoff Holocaust Archive at Yale University.

Very few of the people who survived the Shoah and have given their testimony for posterity served as soldiers. The voices of the victims testify to what we have called the civilianization of war. Genocide is the logical and terrifying outcome of the process whereby the boundary between military and civilian targets in war is erased. We have noted already that international war in the first half of the twentieth century mutated into subnational and transnational warfare in the second half. These new forms of warfare led to what may be termed domestic genocide of the kind that occurred in Cambodia and Rwanda and to civil war genocide of the kind that occurred in the former Yugoslavia. Each produced war crimes trials; each created a new population of moral witnesses who spoke to the yet unknowing world about these atrocities. Their voices matter.

The cruelties of war have spread so widely over the globe that there are and will be moral witnesses speaking of what they have endured in all continents and in many languages. We have gone beyond a purely Eurocentric approach to this element in the cultural history of war. In Guatemala, Honduras, the Congo, in China, Australia, and East Timor, in Syria and Palestine, there are survivors today who make it their life's work to tell the tales of their lives and their people and the suffering they have endured. Most of them have never served in an army, but they are all soldiers of the truth, their truth. The testimony of victims of violence and war is now an integral part of the literary landscape of the contemporary world.

THE CULTURAL HISTORY OF FAMILIES IN WARTIME

10 Families at War

War tears families apart and reconfigures them in ways that make it possible for at least some survivors of the violence of war to put their lives together again thereafter. In this first portion of this section, we consider the ways war affects family formation. We then turn to the role of the state in supporting families.

Marriage

While family life today (2022) goes beyond the conventional pairing of a man and a woman, in the past century the two most important questions in family formation were, at what age do men and women get married for the first time, and at what age do they decide to have children? War has shaped the answers people all over the world have given to those questions.

The decision to go to war took most people by surprise in 1914. In the initial months of the war, many people who had intended to get married in the future brought that date forward. In part, this was to create a home to which to return; in part, it ensured that a wife would have a legal claim for a pension should her husband be killed. After this rush to the altar in 1914 came a dip in the number of marriages contracted over the following four years. After the Armistice, there was another surge of marriages, mostly deferred, and therefore a form of compensation for the enforced separations of the war years.

Over the war decade of 1914–24, the average number of marriages per year was not much above the decade before the war. But there was a change in marriage patterns that directly reflected the heavy casualties of the war years. The age structure of military losses hit very hard the male age group 18–30. These were young, mostly unmarried men. The high death rate among them meant that women had to marry men much older than they were in order to avoid celibacy. That was the case especially in France. In Britain, it was not the age but the social status of marriage partners that changed. The middle and upper classes, from which the officer corps was selected, suffered much higher casualty rates than did working-class men. Thus middle-class women had to adjust their marriage patterns and to accept as husbands men who were at or below their social status in order to avoid celibacy. There is evidence too that women found husbands who had been born in distant parts of Britain; the mobilization of both men and women in war industry thus enlarged the cohort of potential marriage partners.[39]

There is a myth that there was a generation of celibate women whose potential partners had been killed in the war. There were indeed people who fit this description, but for the vast majority of the female population, celibacy was a state to be avoided at all costs. In rural society, it meant dependency on fathers, a mixed blessing for many. Thus shifting the age and social structure of marriage partners made sense.

After the First World War, and more spectacularly after the Second World War, there was a sharp increase in the divorce rate. Part of the source of this inflection was wartime separation; part of it was the realization that some of the rushed marriages of the outbreak of war were unsustainable. In both postwar periods, the costs of divorce proceedings put them out of the reach of the poor, but not of middle-class women seeking freedom, which was very frequently the freedom to remarry.

After the Second World War, in many industrialized countries, a postwar baby boom occurred. Demographers have shown that the source of the major rise in fertility in the period 1945–55 was a decrease in the average age of first

---

[39] Jay Winter, *The Great War and the British people* (London: Macmillan, 1985), ch. 7.

marriage and in the proportion of women who never married at all.[40] The countries that registered the most spectacular increases in fertility in the years 1945–60 shared these trends. They were the United States, Canada, Australia, and New Zealand. In Europe, east and west, there was a smaller baby boom, perhaps best described as a boomlet. Its sources were the same but, in some cases, notably France, the rise in fertility began during the war itself. The Second World War contributed to these developments in a number of ways. The first is that in the immediate postwar years, there was a labor shortage and little or no unemployment.

Rebuilt housing accommodated new families and so did new social services and transfer payments we now summarize under the heading of the welfare state. A subtler element in this story may have been the search for the relative security of domesticity after such an extended period of international war. Single women were particularly vulnerable in war; in its aftermath, getting married was a "normal" thing to do. Even rocky marriages may have appeared to offer more protection for young women than did staying single. We know that the key variable was the propensity of women under the age of twenty-five to marry early and to have children relatively early. Consequently, we need to explore further the attitudes of these women to uncover the origins of the baby boom in different regional and national settings.

Families, War, and the Welfare State

The well-being of families took on new importance in an era of mass conscription. From the late nineteenth century on, producing a healthy generation of new recruits reinforced support for measures of health insurance and healthcare first in Germany, then in Britain, and, after 1945, throughout Europe.

Soldiers signed a kind of social contract when they joined up. If they were injured or killed, they or their families would be supported by the state. After 1914, this understanding underwrote separation allowances in Britain, enabling men to volunteer for service without worrying about how their families would survive without them. Here the state became the surrogate man of the house, and occasionally Victorian ideas about morality led to disputes about whether such payments should be made to women whose morality was questionable. More importantly, these weekly payments were made directly to women. The improvement in the living standards of the working class in general and the poorest among them in particular was due in part to these payments and in part to opportunities for paid labor outside the home women enjoyed in wartime.

---

[40] Samir M. Farid, Cohort nuptiality in England and Wales, *Population Studies*, 30, 1 (March 1976), pp. 137–51.

During and after the war, there were provisions for disability pensions for disabled men and widows' pensions. Cost-conscious bureaucrats operated parsimoniously in almost all circumstances, reducing when possible the payment the state had promised to make. One important distinction was between France and the Anglo-Saxon countries. In France, when a veteran made a claim for a disability pension, that claim was taken as true. If administrators wanted to challenge it on the grounds that the disability was not war-related, then they could do so. But in the Anglo-Saxon countries throughout the twentieth century, the burden of proof that a disability was not the result of a preexisting condition rested on the shoulders of the veteran. This burden reduced substantially the chances that an ex-soldier's claim would be granted.

The French pensions system had one additional feature lacking elsewhere. Children of fathers who had died in active service had the right to be named *Pupilles de la Nation*, or wards of the state. They received grants to buy land, a prerequisite for setting up a farm and a family, as well as other benefits. Among perennial worries that the French birth rate was too low to provide a healthy new generation of recruits, this *largesse* reflected strategic more than humanitarian concerns.

In two respects, provision for veterans in the United States after the Second World War was particularly generous. First, the GI Bill, or, more formally, the Servicemen's Readjustment Act of 1944, gave vets loans to start businesses, low-cost mortgages, unemployment insurance for a year, and life insurance. More than two million men had their college education paid for by the GI Bill, which also funded training for more than five million more vets. Racial discrimination ensured that African-Americans benefited less from these provisions than did their white fellow vets. As Ira Katznelson put it, the GI Bill was "affirmative action for whites."[41]

Other vets were not so lucky. From the early days of the Soviet regime, disabled men had to fight for their rights to a pension, and they were later marginalized by Stalin. The war pensions available under Weimar were more generous than those in interwar Britain, but inflation reduced their real value to the vanishing point. The British expected private philanthropy to supplement state benefits.[42] After 1945, the levels of care and payments available to German war invalids were below those of the interwar period; extirpating the legacy of

---

[41] Ira Katznelson, *When affirmative action was white* (New York: W. W. Norton, 2005), p. 140.

[42] Deborah Cohen, *The war come home: Disabled veterans in Britain and Germany, 1914–1939* (Berkeley: University of California Press, 2001).

German militarism was the occupiers' intention.[43] The same was true in occupied Japan.[44] In China, a policy of ensuring that the material conditions of war veterans did not fall below the national average was handled by local government officials with varying results.

Family Narratives of War, Separation, and Loss

To understand the fate of families at war is to enter the history of emotions. There are thousands of collections of letters and photographs exchanged in wartime that tell us much about how soldiers and their families endured war. Many such letters are banal; some soldiers sound like tourists. After all, they were indeed seeing the world. In other cases, the worries and fears seeped through the lines, even when both sides wanted to show how strong they were.

For children, the war began when their fathers joined up; it ended when they returned. This period of separation was marked by powerful emotions, which is hardly surprising. What was different after 1914 in Europe was the public display of emotion. In some cases, seeing men and women crying in public marked a breach in an unwritten code of social restraint, blurring the line between private and public expressions of strong emotions. Millions of letters were exchanged between front and home every day of the Great War. Children contributed to this epistolary avalanche. In response, soldiers from rural families affirmed their role as head of the family with news and advice about the farm. In many cases, fathers wrote of their love for their children, perhaps for the first time. New codes of emotional exchange emerged in some places between fathers and children. Soldiers sent letters to be read should they not return. At times they spoke of how land or property should be divided; at times they indirectly asked children to forgive them for having abandoned them.[45] Letters between husbands and wives traversed the same territory of hidden and not-so-hidden anxiety. After the war, these letters and photographs became relics of time past. When soldiers died on active service, they took on a special aura. Some families continued to celebrate the birthdays of those who were no longer there. Their names were on war memorials in villages and in many parts of the world. Multiple names told of families hit by the loss of more than one man.

---

[43] James M. Diehl, Change and continuity in the treatment of German *Kriegsopfer*, *Central European History*, 18, 2 (June 1985), pp. 170–87.

[44] Fujiwara Tetsuya, Disabled war veterans during the Allied occupation of Japan, trans. by Ruselle Meade, *SOAS Occasional Translations in Japanese Studies* (3) 2012. www.soas.ac.uk/jrc/translations/file76257.pdf

[45] Manon Pignot, Children, in *The Cambridge History of the First World War*, vol. 3, ed. by Jay Winter (Cambridge: Cambridge University Press, 2014), p. 37.

When armies demobilize, starting family life again is always a challenge. Some soldiers had great difficulty in sharing their war stories with their families and preferred the company of fellow vets. Some chose silence and enclosed their war memories in locked compartments to which only they had the key. What we term the civilianization of war slowly broke down the gender divide between men who went to war and women who stayed home. Women's war narratives, including those of people who served in uniform, have thrown essential light on the cultural history of war all over the world.

Part of the reason for such gender equality in storytelling is related to the overlap between war and genocide. This was especially true after 1945. There was a time lag between the end of the war and the period in the 1970s and after when the voices of the survivors of the Shoah finally were heard. The first Holocaust research center was established in Jerusalem in 1953. It is called Yad Vashem, a name taken from a verse in the book of Isaiah to give a memorial and a name to all those murdered in the Shoah. It opened in 1957. It took another thirty years for what we now call Holocaust memory to become an integral part of the story of the Second World War. By the 1980s, a new technology of video recording and retrieval of testimonies made it possible for many groups and institutions to construct their own Holocaust video archives. By then, the population of survivors had reached advanced ages; the majority were women. It was therefore inevitable that the voice in which the collective story of the Shoah was told was that of a woman. Most war museums spoke with a masculine voice; archives and museums of the Shoah were different.

One of the most important features of these archives was how they captured what we now call the traumatic memory of war. By using the term *trauma*, most people refer to a life-threatening set of events not assimilable in conventional autobiographical terms. Retrieving such memories is difficult because they do not form part of a linear story; many facets are dissociated, shadowy, elusive. The emotional charge of trying to put these elements together can be painful and at times overwhelming.

One group of scholars claims that those passing through trauma cannot inscribe memory traces of them in their minds; others say that traumatic memories are like all other memories. Those oppressed by painful recollections choose to lock them up or hide them away. They are there but become inaccessible. This second group has the majority of scientific opinion on its side.[46] Those who retain traumatic memories of the Shoah, like survivors of the Armenian

---

[46] Richard J. McNally, Debunking myths about trauma and memory, *Canadian Journal of Psychiatry*, 1, 13 (November 2005), pp. 817–22.

Figure 20 Mothers of the Plaza de Mayo, Buenos Aires, Argentina, demonstrating to find the truth about the "disappeared."
Source: Photo by Majority World/Universal Images Group via Getty Images

genocide, may be able to tell the story only after a significant period of time. In some cases, it is possible for survivors to tell what happened to them only to their grandchildren. Survivors wanted to protect their children from these stories and give them a chance to lead normal lives. But as survivors age and the memories of terrible times return, they may form a bond with grandchildren stronger than the one they share with the difficult generation in the middle. Then grandchildren hear stories never told before.[47] This same multigenerational transmission of war stories occurred among soldiers and their descendants. In both cases, the story of war told in public has always been only part of a broader narrative, only some of which we hear. For many who survive it, war indeed is beyond words.

The Dirty War waged by Argentine authorities in the 1970s and early 1980s led a group of women to perform their traumatic memories in public. In front of the Casa Rosada, the president's residence in Buenos Aires, mothers met every Thursday between 1977 and 2006. They demanded to be told what had happened to their sons and daughters who disappeared during the Dirty War. In Figure 20, we see these mothers of the Plaza de Mayo demonstrating to be told

---

[47] For just one case in point, see Peter Balakian, *The black dog of fate: An American son uncovers his Armenian past* (New York: Broadway, 1997).

the truth about what happened to their "disappeared" children. Other women formed a parallel association, the Grandmothers of the Plaza de Mayo. They continue to press for information on babies stolen from prisoners and then adopted by regime supporters. As of 2019, 130 such children (now adults) have been found and have learned what had happened to them.

Gender and War: Violence against Women

So far we have approached the cultural history of families in wartime in terms of family formation, the role of the state in providing material support for soldiers and their families, and forms of storytelling that emerged from war. There is another domain of the story of families in wartime that has only recently received the attention it deserves. That subject is sexual violence against women in war. Such violence is a crime against individual women and a crime against their families. Men are defined in patriarchal societies in terms of their activities outside the home; women are defined by what they do inside the home. Every victim of sexual violence is someone's mother, wife, sister, or daughter. That is why sexual violence against women in war is an even more egregious affront to family life than the violence men endure in combat. In Figure 21, we see Mary, aged fifteen, who was raped and forced into sex work by the Lord's Resistance Army in Uganda. Her face speaks eloquently of the abomination of sexual violence in war.

Like everything else about war in the twentieth century, this subject is both very old and very new. Rape is part of the story of war in the classics. In our own times, the incidence of sexual violence inflicted on women in wartime has not

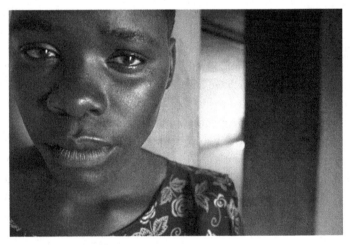

Figure 21 Mary, aged fifteen, raped by the Lord's Resistance Army in Uganda.
Source: Photo by Alvaro Ybarra Zavala/Edit by Getty Images

only grown exponentially, it has also been instrumentalized as a weapon of war. Rape is now recognized as a crime in international law. Depending on circumstances, rape is now prosecuted as a war crime, a crime against humanity, and an act contributing to genocide.

The criminalization in international law of rape in wartime as a form of degradation and torture sufficiently serious to be named a crime against humanity goes well beyond domestic criminal law. This juridical distinction may disappear someday, but the recognition of rape as a crime in international law highlights the political context in which it takes place. Mass rape has become a political weapon, aiming not only at the body of the violated woman but also at her family and her people as a whole.

Violence against women has been an expression of racial prejudice for centuries. In 1914, propagandists interpreted the invasion of the enemy as a form of rape easily expressed in lurid posters. It was true that rape occurred in many theaters of military operations in the First World War. Rapists were punished under military law in many cases. Where rape became part of the civilianization of war, part of the deliberate extension of violence to civilians, it opened a new phase in the history of war crimes. Rape was part of the degradation and destruction of the Armenian people in the course of the genocide set in motion by the ruling triumvirate in control of the Ottoman Turkish war effort in 1915.

The racialization of warfare was manifest in the Japanese treatment of Chinese civilians in Nanjing in 1937. An army enraged by casualties suffered in combat took out its anger on the bodies of women; no one knows precisely how many were raped and murdered in this paroxysm of violence in December 1937. Japanese racialism lay behind the system of forced prostitution of Korean "comfort women" both before and during the war. Making women pay for the crimes "their men" committed elsewhere was evident in Berlin in 1945. Soviet troops took out on the bodies of the women of Berlin their rage at the Nazis' treatment of civilians in Russia during the war.

The historian George Mosse developed the idea of the brutalization of combat troops in wartime. That notion has been used to account for rape in the Second World War by other troops. American GIs committed thousands of rapes while liberating France in 1944. Moroccan troops serving with the Allies in Italy became infamous as sexual predators in the Italian countryside. The Italian term *Marrochinate* was coined for their criminal acts, which went largely unpunished. There are similar accounts of rape in Vietnam by American troops fighting a losing war far from home. Were soldiers who raped simply civilian rapists in uniform who used their status and weapons to torture women? Or did the brutality of military life inject into those who fought a version of masculinity shot through with sadism? The answer probably lies somewhere between these two possibilities.

In the last decade of the twentieth century, rape in wartime was recognized finally as part of an array of sexual crimes committed with political motives during periods of civil war. This advance in jurisprudence was significant in a number of ways. First, it put to rest the old adage that rape happens in war, a natural act almost like rainfall. Second, it located rape within an array of practices aiming at either destroying a particular ethnic group or so terrifying its members that they flee disputed territory.

The two civil wars in which mass rape occurred were in the former Yugoslavia and in Rwanda. When the federation that made up Yugoslavia fell apart, a civil war between Bosnian Serbs and Muslims broke out in Bosnia. In 1992, there were reports that Bosnian Serb military and paramilitary groups had set up rape camps in which Bosnian women were imprisoned. In total perhaps twenty thousand women were raped. The purpose was both torture and the ethnic cleansing of Muslims from Bosnia.

Two years later, in Rwanda, mass rape was used as a tool of genocide. Hutu militants mobilized killing squads targeting the Tutsi population. Estimates vary, but all agree that hundreds of thousands of Tutsi women and children were mutilated, raped, and murdered in 1994.

In both Rwanda and the former Yugoslavia, international tribunals were set up to bring these crimes and these criminals to justice. In Figure 22, we see a number of men standing before the International Criminal Court in Arusha facing accusations of responsibility for genocide in Rwanda.

It was in this context that rape was recognized as a war crime, a crime against humanity, and a crime in the pursuance of genocide. In 1998, the International Criminal Tribunal for Rwanda, set up at Arusha, Tanzania, in 1994, reached the judgment that the crime of rape should be recognized as a means of perpetrating genocide. In the same year, 1998, the International Tribunal for the former Yugoslavia found that acts of rape may constitute torture under customary international law. In a number of trials of Serbs accused of acts of sexual violence committed during the civil war, the court found that rape was used to enforce a policy of expulsion through terror.

In the last decade of the twentieth century, civil war turned sexual crimes into political acts. In both Bosnia and Rwanda, systematic sexual assaults on women occurred as part of a war effort aiming at ethnic cleansing. That use of rape for political purposes was criminalized in international law in two tribunals meeting in the years just before the new century. Part of the force behind these judgments was a recognition that rape is a crime not only against women but against all of us. The right to family life is inscribed in the Universal Declaration

Figure 22 Accused men appearing before the International Criminal Court for Rwanda, Arusha, Tanzania.

Source: Photo by Christophe Calais/Corbis via Getty Images

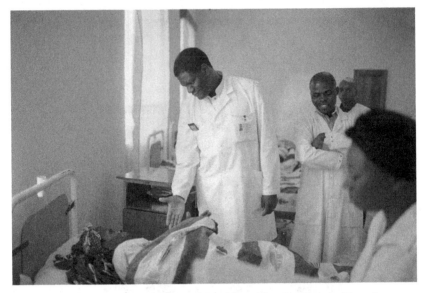

Figure 23 Dr. Denis Mukwege at the Panzi Hospital for victims of rape,
Bukavu, the Democratic Republic of the Congo.
Source: Photo by Per-Anders Pettersson/Getty Images

of Human Rights of 1948. Slavery and torture are outlawed in the same
document. It took fifty years before international law took account of rape as
an act of war and therefore an abomination that had to be proscribed. That is one
step toward defending family life from the endemic political violence of the
world in which we live.

Dr. Denis Mukwege won the Nobel Peace Prize in 2018. He was honored for
his work in Panzi Hospital, in Bukava, the Democratic Republic of the Congo,
in treating victims of rape in armed conflict. In Figure 23, we see him on a ward
round in his hospital. We are a long way from ending the use of sexual violence
as a weapon of war, but people like Mukwege keep that hope alive.

11 The Double Helix

Gender is a set of codes, symbolic, legal, political, and economic, that govern
the relations of men and women. The subject of gender is power, and that power
is almost always tilted toward men. Patriarchy is the set of social relations
expressing this inequality in the relation between men and women. Patriarchy
rests on the belief that the value of the life of a male is greater than the value of
the life of a female. Sexual violence both arises from and is tolerated in societies
that accept this vicious principle.

The effect of warfare is almost always to deepen patriarchy and its tilt toward male power. However, gender is not a linear but a dialectical relationship. Patrice and Margaret Higonnet have captured this truth in their introduction to a seminal collection of essays they published on gender and war.[48] They described the field of force in gender relations as resembling a double helix in molecular biology. The dominance of the male is structural. Within that space male and female subject positions circle around each other, and when there is a change in the status of women, there occurs a shift in the position of men that tends to stabilize the system. Women advance, but the distance between them and that of men remains roughly the same. This has been the case in wartime throughout the twentieth century.

The Great War

Since gender relations focus on power, when power hierarchies in politics are challenged, so are gender relations. The invasion of a country, propagandists everywhere proclaimed, is like rape; the crime needs to be avenged and the national army is the agent of that punishment. Should the invader prevail, even for limited periods, the crime goes unpunished and the defeated males are humiliated. Hence in the many areas that wound up under enemy occupation in the First World War, the impotence of the local indigenous males is built into the fact of occupation. That happened in Belgium, France, Serbia, and East Prussia in 1914, in Serbia again, Turkey, and Russia in 1915, in Serbia, Bulgaria, and Greece in 1917, and in Russia again in 1918.

Fighting did not cease everywhere on November 11. The war against Germany and Austria-Hungary came to an end with Allied victory. But the collapse of the Russian empire and the outbreak of the Bolshevik Revolution opened a Pandora's box of armed conflict, including civil wars, wars of national independence, class wars, and wars targeting religious minorities, in particular Jews and the Armenian and Greek-Orthodox communities in Anatolia. In every single one of these postwar conflicts, sexual violence accompanied the upheaval of ordinary life.

Anxiety accompanied the mobilization of armies too. It was not only familial fears for the well-being of their men, but their men's fears of losing their authority at home that counted. That is why so many soldiers' letters are full of instructions; the implicit assumption is that women cannot make the right

---

[48] Margaret Higonnet and Patrice Higonnet, The double helix, in *Behind the lines: Gender and the two world wars*, ed. by Margaret Higonnet, Jane Jenson, Sonya Michel, and Margaret Collins Weitz (New Haven, CT: Yale University Press, 1987), pp. 31–50.

decisions needed to keep the farm in order. Male fantasies about women's
infidelities are abundant in soldiers' newspapers. This was a time-honored
theme in prewar theater and popular literature, but in reading the wartime
popular press and the weeklies soldiers produced themselves, soldiers could
hide their worries in convivial laughter.

The arrival on the Western Front of African soldiers added a racial
element to this simmering pot of male anxieties. In the Parisian satiric
newspaper *La Baïonnette* of August 3, 1917, there is a send up of the
French practice of women cheering up soldiers by sending them letters.
These letter writers were called Marraines or godmothers. The newspaper
saw through that conceit and asked its readers to imagine what happened
when the letter writer met the letter reader, when he was black. His response
was disappointment: he dreamt of meeting a blond, says the caption to
Figure 24.

The same Parisian weekly printed another bit of anxious humor on May 1,
1917, when the French army was in the early stages of mutiny. By then

Figure 24 "And I was expecting a blonde," *La Baïonnette*, August 3, 1917

Figure 25 "Merry Widows," *La Baïonnette*, May 1, 1917

roughly eight hundred thousand Frenchmen had been killed. What was the fate of the widows among their wives? They wore widows' clothes, but tried to enjoy themselves anyway. As we see in Figure 25, the drawing is entitled "Merry Widows."[49]

Another set of traces of these wartime worries about gender may be found in cinema. In the great film of Jean Renoir entitled *The Grand Illusion*, French prisoners of war offer their captors a drag entertainment. They dress up in women's clothes and make light of the fact that they haven't seen women for years. *Travestie* was the French word for cross-dressing; the word can mean

---

[49] For a discussion of gender anxiety in war, see Jay Winter, War and anxiety in 1917, in *The myriad legacies of 1917: A year of war and revolution*, ed. by Maartje Abbenhuis, Neill Atkinson, Kingsley Baird, and Gail Romano (London: Palgrave Macmillan, 2018), pp. 13–33.

distortion, and it was the distortion of sex roles in wartime that caused unease in many soldiers' minds.

This distortion may help explain the hypermasculinity of war propaganda. Turning all men into muscular heroes was one way of rallying public opinion around the flag. It was also a way of saying that the patriarchic order in which these men in uniform had lived before the war would be there on their return.

In a host of ways, we can see that mass mobilization and mass casualties destabilized gender roles and patriarchy in the First World War. The state recognized the difficulty of men looking after their families in the early months of the war. Separation allowances were paid to women to ensure that no family would be in penury because of mobilization. The state stood in place of the male wage earner and enabled men to go off to war without fearing that their families would go hungry.

When stalemate set in in 1915, there was a shift of the female labor force out of textiles and into heavy manufacturing, particularly in the munitions industries. This development further destabilized gender relations. Women's pay increased and those who were married had full control over the family income in wartime. In France, male wages were calculated as being sufficient for the man to support his family. Would male wages now be cut because women were earning their own living?

We see here the complex web of changes in the wartime sexual division of labor that made it difficult for men to believe that they could return to the homes and authority they had had before the war. War provided many similar vectors of change that after the war were met by equal and at least as powerful vectors of restoration. That is what the double helix metaphor captures. In Lenin's language, women took two steps forward in wartime, in work, and in society as a whole. They had to change their lives to do their bit for the war effort. But in the aftermath of war, women took two steps backward. The first was to vacate "male" jobs and the second was to return to hearth and home and prepare both for the returning soldiers. This was as true in the victorious countries as in those that lost the war.

Another irritant to patriarchy was political. During the First World War, many prominent women joined peace movements. In 1915, there was a meeting in neutral Netherlands of the Women's International League of Peace and Freedom. One of its leaders was Jane Addams, an American progressive. Many women who broke ranks with the majority supporting the war were persecuted in wartime. Like Sylvia Pankhurst in Britain, Rosa Luxemburg, a founder of the German Communist Party, spent long stretches in jail. After the war, Luxemburg was murdered by paramilitary troops. In Russia, Alexandra

Kollontai spoke up for women's rights; so did Emma Goldman in the United States.

Some believed that the granting of votes to women in a number of countries at the end of the First World War was a reward for their contribution to the war effort. This is only partly true. The male electorate also expanded at the end of the war as a recognition of their military service, reenforcing the Higonnets' notion that war changed politics but maintained the distance between the male and female roles in the political order.

One woman who believed that women's roles had changed during the war was Vera Britten. Her 1933 memoir, *Testament of Youth*, told of her sense of outrage at the suffering she saw as a Voluntary Aid Detachment nurse in the First World War and of her commitment, because of what she had seen, to speak out against war. A wider engagement of women in politics, domestic and international, is one reason many women believed that the war had given them a voice they had not had before 1914. This claim was true but needs to be tempered by the Higonnets' argument that what matters is the distance between the subject position of men and women in a traditional society like Britain or elsewhere.

The Second World War

The Bolshevik Revolution set in motion a multinational counterrevolution of the right. In its most radical form in Germany, the Nazi Party conjured up a world conspiracy of Bolsheviks and Jews that had not only snatched victory from Germany in 1918 (a blatant lie) but threatened to destroy the German people thereafter. National assertion after humiliation was the cry that accompanied the arrival of fascists in power in 1922 in Italy. A war to push back the menace of atheism and Bolshevism opened with the attempted seizure of power by nationalist soldiers in Spain in July 1936. In every one of these right-wing movements, and in many of their followers elsewhere, a hypermasculine conservatism flourished. The fact that roughly half of those who voted for Hitler were women suggests that this message appealed to both men and women.

For the Nazis, racial purity meant a fortification of the German family. There was a tension from the start between the belief that women's place was in the home and the need for expanding the female labor force to contribute to German rearmament. That tension was never resolved. But in the public sphere, and in almost all of its symbolic language, women were not primarily workers but the carriers of the future master race. The waging of war after 1939 forced even the Nazis to consider compromising on the issue of gender roles. Women had to be mobilized too. Elsewhere, the same destabilization of gender roles followed the same path as in the First World War. What differentiated the two conflicts was air war. Until 1944, more civilians than soldiers died in Britain. The toll taken by the destruction of Warsaw in 1939 and Rotterdam and Coventry in 1940 from the air was small in comparison to the whirlwind that hit Europe from the air thereafter.

Propaganda campaigns in every country showed the stolid steadfastness of women in wartime. But they never conscripted women as did both Britain and the Soviet Union. In Hitler's Germany, women's role in perpetuating the race came first. The heroic male remained the pillar of the nation. Elsewhere in Europe and beyond, women played a vital role in the war effort of all combatant countries. Women served in every branch of the Soviet forces. They were pivotal members of every resistance group throughout the continent. Some espionage networks were run by women, for instance the Red Orchestra. They served in China and in Africa. Thousands of women worked at Bletchley Park in Britain to break German coded communications. But in the multiple narratives that emerged from the war, men still took center stage.

It could not have been otherwise. The disruption of or destruction of family life in the Second World War spanned a huge spectrum. At one extreme was genocide. At the other extreme was family separation and a return of women to war factories. Rosie the Riveter was a popular figure, but she represented a destabilization of the double helix of gender that could not be permitted to continue after the war. Male riveters needed their jobs back after the war. A restoration of family life came before any consideration of the rights of women to a life outside of the family, always configured in patriarchal terms.

One set of events in 1945 showed how the tilt toward patriarchy operated to occlude national humiliation. After the withdrawal of German occupying troops from France, women said to have had liaisons with Germans were publicly shamed. They had their hair shorn off by Frenchmen who may or may not have worked in the Resistance. In Figure 26, we see the performance on the bodies of women of the impotence of Frenchmen, too weak on their own to throw out the German occupiers before the arrival of the Allies.[50]

After the war, the family did indeed make a comeback. In many countries after 1945, there was a major increase in the birth rate. In part this was a reflection, as we have seen in Section 10, of the decision of women to marry earlier and to have children earlier than did their mothers. Why did they so decide? One answer is a search for what one historian called a haven in a heartless world. That is no doubt an idealized vision of the inevitable turbulence built into family life, but the phrase does capture the sense that domesticity was defined as a protected realm;

---

[50] Fabrice Virgili, *La France "virile": Des femmes tondues à la Libération* (Paris: Payot, 2000).

Figure 26 French women suspected of having taken German lovers during the Occupation, humiliated in public, 1945.
Source: Photo by Three Lions/Getty Images

better to live in it than alone in the harsh environment most of the world had known from 1939 to 1945. It is true that this baby boom was most marked in countries that had not seen fighting on their own soil – the United States, Canada, Australia, and New Zealand. But there was a smaller but still real baby boom on the European continent.

At the same time, a number of combatant countries experienced historically high economic growth. The replacement of capital was necessary and there were more jobs on offer than there were people to fill them – a striking shift from the interwar years. But there was another explanation for the baby boom. Many combatant countries nationalized their health service systems. In part this was a reflection of long-term trends, but it also showed a commitment to health as a commitment to the future. In Western Europe, such innovations were responses to unwelcome comparisons with the rights offered citizens of the communist east. After the end of the war, better jobs, better housing, better healthcare were the realities that persuaded women to choose to marry early and to start their families at young ages.

The consumer revolution that followed was reinforced by popular images of domesticity that benefited the light consumer durable industries. Homemaking became a patriotic act and served to restore patriarchy to its traditional place. And yet the lessons of wartime, and in particular of women's political activism in the two world wars, were not lost. The daughters of the war generation were the women of 1968. They brought a new woman's movement to life, one with us still.

Asymmetric Wars and Gender after 1950

The period after 1950 was one in which war changed, but the effect of war on patriarchy remained the same. Part of the reason was the hypermasculine character of most movements for national liberation. Women played essential roles in most if not all of them, but when new nations emerged, it was to create a social order in which masculine power prevailed.

The wars of the post-1950 period coincided with the emergence of a new worldwide human rights movement. Always women's rights were interpolated within the corpus of human rights. But once again, always, when there was a choice between women's rights and human rights, women's rights lost out. The struggle for women to have the right to abortion was a matter of liberation. But in all too many cases, emerging nations truncated the liberation of women in order to create a stable political and social order in the aftermath of independence.

The story of women's role during and after the fight for independence in Algeria can stand for many others. The Front for the Liberation of the Nation (FLN) led the struggle for independence. Its stance for the international press was that by fighting for freedom, Algerian women were fighting for equality in the new Algeria. The reality was more complex. French strategy to hold on to Algeria included steps to improve women's education, voting rights, the right to appear in public without a veil, access to healthcare, and jobs. The FLN opposed these measures as a violation of Islam. This conservative position effectively neutralized the work of another branch of the liberation movement. The psychologist Franz Fanon spoke out on this issue and envisaged radical changes in the role of women in independent Algeria.[51]

Nothing of the kind happened after 1962. Though more than two thousand women were arrested and many were tortured and raped, the role of women in the fight for freedom was played down after the war. Women's rights were low priority as the regime turned against anything deemed Western and therefore

---

[51] Adrienne Leonhardt, Between two jailers: Women's experience during colonialism, war, and independence in Algeria, *Anthós*, 5, 1 (2013), pp. 43–54.

colonial. Strict marriage laws, inaction over sexual violence against women, forced veiling, and the banning of birth control followed.

The story of women in Vietnam after the war for independence shows some similar features to that of Algeria. There is the same downplaying of the military role of women in the war effort. The Ho Chi Minh Trail was the conduit for moving essential supplies south, and women made it work. In postwar commemorative practices, there is the same forgetting of women's role in winning the war, the same hypermasculine representation of the victorious nation. Heonik Kwon has shown, though, that there was a difference. On the domestic level, below the radar of the Communist Party, women played an essential role in rituals of mourning the dead. Women put to rest what he calls the ghosts of Vietnam, the millions of people who were buried far from home or who simply disappeared.[52] Kwon has shown that women played a similar role in Korea, long after the fighting ended in 1953.[53]

There was more continuity in the fight for gender equality in South Africa before and after the fall of apartheid. Women's role in the struggle was not occluded, and a substantial number of women were and are active in South African political life. Still, women's activism has faded since independence and sexual violence remains rampant. The same is true in India and in other Asian countries after independence.

An explanation for this pattern of engagement with women's rights during the struggle for independence and an abandonment of these commitments thereafter lies in the Higonnets' image of the double helix. The end of colonialism benefited women as well as men, but the political and economic elites who came to power in most countries took steps to stabilize their new regimes by either dropping campaigns for women's rights or subsuming them under the portmanteau of development. Our conclusion is that wars against colonialism are no different than world wars or national wars. They start out with the dream of creating a new society and wind up configuring an old one with a new name. It is time to put to rest the old shibboleth that war liberates women. It very rarely does so. What happens during and after war is a restructuring of a double helix and a recalibration of the continuing distance between the power men and women have to exercise freedom.

12 Flight

The thirty years before the First World War form one of the most remarkable periods in the history of international migration. Perhaps thirty million people

---

[52] Heonik Kwon, *Ghosts of war in Vietnam* (Cambridge: Cambridge University Press, 2008).
[53] Kwon, *After the Korean War.*

moved from East to West, through European ports and cities, and traversed the Atlantic Ocean. Most settled in Western Europe or North America, though a substantial wave of people landed in South America too.

That vast migratory wave came to an end in 1914. It was replaced by a similarly huge movement of people who sought a new life, not primarily because of poverty or domestic persecution, but because of war. War-related famine and disease added millions to this displaced population. The historian Peter Gatrell has drawn attention in his seminal scholarship on this period to a word coined in the nineteenth century to describe the vast space in which such people moved and lived. It was called "refugeedom."[54]

The Great War

What made the Great War a watershed in the history of refugeedom was the intersection of war and revolution in 1917. Both accelerated the flow of populations fleeing armed conflict and led to the end of unrestricted entry into the United States. The Johnson-Reed Act, signed into law in 1924, sharply reduced the number of immigrants allowed into the United States from Europe and even more drastically cut the number of those allowed in from Asia. The quotas were aimed at preserving the ethnic stock of the United States as it had been before the war. In particular, the law targeted potential migrants from Eastern and Southern Europe who, according to the eugenic clichés of the day, brought with them and propagated disease and revolutionary ideas.

An avalanche of refugees accompanied the outbreak of the war. And that was hardly surprising, since the fighting in 1914 was even bloodier than the years of stalemate that followed; roughly one million men died in combat in the five months from August to December 1914. Perhaps one million of Belgium's eight million people fled their country. At least as many fled from Serbia in the first year of the war. Military defeat sent several hundred thousand Serb troops and civilians over the mountains into Albania in winter 1915. Loss of life in Serbia was staggering. Military losses there were proportionately the highest of all nations in the war; roughly 35 percent of those in Serb uniforms died during the conflict. War-related civilian deaths were estimated at more than half a million. Roughly one hundred and fifty thousand were victims of a typhus epidemic in 1915.[55] Figure 27 shows some of these Serbian refugees in flight from the war in 1915.

---

[54] Peter Gatrell, *The making of the modern refugee* (Oxford: Oxford University Press, 2013); Peter Gatrell, War, refugeedom, revolution, *Cahiers du Monde russe*, 58, 1/2; 1917: Historiographie, dynamiques révolutionnaires et mémoires contestées (January–June 2017), pp. 123–46.

[55] Dušan T. Bataković, Serbia's effort in the Great War: Testimonies, commemorations, interpretations, in *Cent ans après: La Mémoire de la première guerre mondiale,* ed. by Elli Lemonidou (Athens: Ecole Française d'Athènes, 2020), pp. 157–85.

Figure 27 Serbian refugees in flight, 1915.
Source: Photo by Hulton Archive/Getty Images

The year 1915 was a disaster as well for the Jewish population of Eastern Europe. Those who lived in the Pale of Settlement were displaced by the Russian army after it had suffered setbacks in the first year of the war. The Russian High Command suspected Jewish solidarity with their German and Austro-Hungarian adversaries and uprooted roughly half a million people from their homes. Murder, rape, hunger, and epidemic disease followed.[56] No one knows how many died. As we have noted in Section 6, this episode of persecution became known to the Yiddish-speaking population as the "Drittr Hurban," the third destruction of the Jewish world, as terrible as the two moments when the Temple in Jerusalem was destroyed.[57] Jewish refugees streamed into major cities in Vienna, Prague, and Warsaw. This massive destabilization of western Russia is part of the story of the unraveling of the czarist regime. After the two revolutions in Russia in 1917, refugee flows were even greater. During the civil war that followed, the defeated White armies and civilians fled south to Constantinople. Others settled in China.

---

[56] Eric Lohr, The Russian army and the Jews: Mass deportation, hostages, and violence during World War I, *Russian Review*, 60, 3 (July 2001), pp. 404–19.

[57] S. Ansky, *The enemy at his pleasure: A journey through the Jewish Pale of Settlement during World War I*, ed. and trans. by Joachim Neugroschel (New York: Metropolitan Books, 2002).

Harbin was essentially a Russian city and Shanghai housed a large Russian community.

Beginning in 1915, a catastrophe of perhaps even greater dimensions occurred in Ottoman Turkey. In Turkey, the Ottoman regime crushed its own citizens. From April 1915, more than one million Armenian civilians died after being forcibly ejected from their homes in Anatolia and force-marched to the Mesopotamian desert and Syria. Nearly one million Armenians became refugees, many living in camps where epidemic disease was rife. Those who survived scattered to all corners of the globe.[58]

Postwar: 1917–39

In the years 1917–23, hundreds of thousands of people were on the move in Eastern Europe and in Asia Minor. The revolutionary regime in Russia abandoned the war in 1917. Millions of soldiers streamed home, determined to claim land in the new order. Further south, another million refugees fled the defeat of the Greek armies destroyed by nationalist forces in Turkey. Armenians joined them in escaping from Anatolia.

In July 1923, the Treaty of Lausanne, ending the First World War in the east, added a new twist to the story of refugeedom. Part of the treaty set in motion a compulsory population exchange. All Greek Orthodox residents of Anatolia, with the exception of those living in Constantinople and some islands, had to leave Turkey; in exchange, all Muslim residents of Greece, with the exception of those living in western Thrace, had to leave Greece. Such movements had happened voluntarily before; what made Lausanne unique is that it made citizenship a function of religion and specified that the targeted religious groups could not return to their former homes. This set a terrible precedent for what we now call ethnic cleansing.[59]

The new League of Nations was committed to the defense of the rights of minorities. But throughout the interwar years, different states either ignored or violated their commitments in this field. By the mid-1930s, when the militarized regimes in Berlin, Rome, and Tokyo had come to power, a new global refugee crisis unfolded.

After 1931, and even more intensely after 1937, millions of Chinese people fled from the advancing Japanese armies. In 1935, Italy's invasion of Ethiopia

---

[58] Peter Gatrell and Jo Laycock, Armenia: The nationalization, internationalization and representation of the refugee crisis, in *Homelands: War, population and statehood in Eastern Europe and Russia, 1918–1924*, ed. by Nick Baron and Peter Gatrell (London: Anthem Press, 2004), pp. 179–200.

[59] Jay Winter, *The day the Great War ended, 24 July 1923: The civilianization of war* (Oxford: Oxford University Press, 2022).

sent streams of African refugees away from the fighting. The same flows followed the outbreak of the Spanish civil war in 1936. Even after the nationalists emerged victorious in 1939, the flight of civilians across the Pyrenees into France and safety continued.

The Second World War

Nazi persecution of Jews after 1933 led to the flight of nearly four hundred thousand Jewish people from Germany and Austria to Britain and other Western European countries. An astonishing array of organizations moved mountains to accommodate these people. Then disaster struck in 1939. With the outbreak of war, these German refugees at a stroke became enemy aliens in countries at war with Germany. When disaster turned into catastrophe after the German breakthroughs of 1940, politicians, including Winston Churchill, fell prey to the delusion that these people harbored German spies. The outcome was the internment of tens of thousands of victims of the Nazis in prison camps in Britain. Many were sent by boat to Canada or Australia to be interned there. As we have already noted, one of those boats, *Arandora Star*, was sunk by a U-boat; seven hundred internees drowned. After the threat of German invasion lifted in 1941, Churchill among others admitted the cruel error of this policy. Over time, these abused refugees were freed; many wound up fighting for Britain and the Allies anyway.[60]

The brutality of the Second World War scattered fleeing civilians to all corners of the world. Thousands of German and Austrian Jews wound up in Shanghai, one of the few places in the world where you did not need a visa to settle. Most of these people had tried to get to the United States but had failed to get a visa. After the war, many realized that dream. Others wound up in Palestine, Australia, and South America.

To understand how refugees survived, we need to enter the cultural lives of refugees themselves. Instead of seeing them as helpless victims, historians have turned to the record of their lives as active creators of art and literature while incarcerated and as active agents of their survival, both during and after the war.[61]

Postwar: 1945–53

The end of the war in Europe left millions of people staggering out of prisons and concentration camps. Many of them had no intention of returning to the

---

[60] Ken Inglis, Seumas Spark, and Jay Winter, *Dunera lives: A visual history* (Melbourne: Monash University Publications, 2018).

[61] Peter Gatrell, Refugees: What's wrong with history? *Journal of Refugee Studies*, 30, 2 (June 2017), pp. 170–89.

states in which they had suffered persecution during the war. Hundreds of thousands had been made stateless – that is, deprived both of citizenship and of nationality – either by the Soviet Union or by Nazi Germany.

The UN addressed this problem in its Convention on Refugees of 1951, which went beyond earlier efforts of the League of Nations to help such people. This document stated that a refugee is a person forced to flee from a country whose legal protections fail him or her. A migrant still has the protection of his or her home country while abroad. Refugees do not have this protection and, for that reason, the UN provides an extraterritorial status for them. In 1967, this status was extended to people all over the world, regardless of when they fled their countries. In both the 1951 and 1967 documents, refugees have the right not to be returned forcibly to their home countries. This provision is now a rule of customary international law.

Three massive refugee crises took place during the immediate postwar years. One was the terrifying wave of ethnic violence accompanying India's independence. On August 15, 1947, partition displaced between ten and twenty million people, whose flight was accompanied by murder on a staggering scale. Perhaps one million people died in this period.

The second was the flight of Palestinian refugees in the wake of the Arab-Israeli war of 1948. Refugees left out of fear; a large number were subject to threats and violence by Israeli forces. By 1949, the UN took responsibility for relief work in Palestine for the seven hundred thousand people who had lost their homes in the war. Seventy years later, it still provides food, shelter, schools, and other assistance for more than four million Palestinians.

The third was the flight of approximately seven hundred thousand people who went south and six hundred thousand who went north during the Korean War of 1950–3. Many remained vulnerable to accusations of disloyalty to the regime they had fled and virtually all lost touch with family members on the other side of the Demilitarized Zone. This story of fractured families is a leitmotif of the history of displaced people throughout the twentieth century and after.[62]

Ethnic Cleansing and Genocide, 1975–95

In three countries, war created the conditions that made genocide possible. After the victory of North Vietnam in 1975, the communist Pol Pot regime in bordering Cambodia turned on its own population of city dwellers and imprisoned, tortured, and murdered up to one-quarter of the population of eight million people. These crimes came to an end only when Vietnamese troops invaded and

---

[62] Kwon, *After the Korean War.*

toppled the regime. Roughly two hundred and seventy thousand people fled the country between 1975 and 1979.

Between 1992 and 1995, Serbian forces battled Croatian and Bosniak forces in the former Yugoslavia. After the end of the conflict, the International Criminal Court for the former Yugoslavia declared that Bosnian Serb killings of Bosnian Muslim men in Srebenice on July 11, 1995, constituted genocide. Other courts absolved the Serbian state of direct responsibility for these crimes. Roughly three hundred and fifty thousand refugees from this war zone wound up in Germany, then heavily engaged in the process of reunification.

The Great Lakes Refugee Crisis is the name given to the parallel flight of two million Rwandans during the genocide of Tutsis by Hutu radicals in 1994. Some of the perpetrators of genocide hid among these refugees. Around one and a half million of them returned home by 1997.

Iraq, Afghanistan, Syria

The overthrow of the Taliban government in Afghanistan and the invasion of Iraq in 2003 created a massive wave of refugees. Estimates go as high as six million displaced Afghans in the first decade of the twenty-first century; most found shelter in Pakistan. The situation in Iraq was similar. Four years after the US-led invasion, there were an estimated four million Iraqi refugees, half in Iraq itself. The Iraqi civil war that followed left three million Iraqis displaced in their own country. In the case of Syria, plagued by civil war since 2012, approximately six million refugees have sought asylum abroad. Figure 28 shows Syrian refugees landing on Lesbos, Greece, in 2020.

The cultural history of what may be termed the multiple civil wars in the Islamic world has still to be written. On one side, radical Islam has taken to extremes anti-imperial and anti-Western tropes that emerged in the aftermath of the First World War. On the other side, Islamophobia has emerged as a major political force in Europe and North America. Muslims have lived on both sides of the Atlantic for generations. Fear of Islam as a threat to the existence of Western nations antedated 2001. After 9/11, there were other suicide attacks in European cities. Following them, anti-Muslim sentiment has fueled a populist revolt against centrist toleration of all immigrants.

In a way, over the past century we have come full circle. In the aftermath of the First World War, immigrants from Eastern and Southern Europe presented threats to the paranoid right in Western Europe and the United States. A century later, the spectre of communism evaporated. In its place, the fear of Islam and of Muslim migrants has gripped many feverish imaginations. Those fleeing the

Figure 28 Syrian refugees land on Lesbos, Greece, 2020.
Source: Photo by Spencer Platt/Getty Images

violence accompanying narco-traffic in Mexico have been similarly vilified. Migrants, President Trump said, are rapists and criminals. The political appeal of such apostles of fear is still considerable.

In 2022, millions of civilians fleeing the Russian invasion of Ukraine have elicited considerable sympathy and material aid from people around the world. They have been welcomed, housed, and fed by neighboring populations in Europe and beyond. The fact that most of these refugees are Christian and white may have helped in the relief of their plight. It is an open question as to whether this moment of solidarity with innocent Ukrainians fleeing war will enhance a more generous reaction in the West to future war-related refugee flows from the nonwhite world.

One source of hope is embedded in this tangled and bloody story of war and refugeedom. Those who have escaped war and persecution have helped create the robust cultural and political life of diasporic communities all over the world. Irish Americans played an important role in the defusing of the Northern Ireland problem, leading to the Good Friday Agreement of 1998. The Armenian diaspora has kept alive the national project a century after great power diplomacy and Turkish military success buried it at Lausanne. Congolese and other Africans play an important role in the political, social, and cultural life of France, Belgium, and other European countries. Abdulrazak Gurnah won the

Nobel Prize for Literature in 2021. He is a native of Zanzibar and is now a British citizen. His citation praised him for "his uncompromising and compassionate penetration of the effects of colonialism and the fate of the refugee in the gulf between cultures and continents."[63] Gurnah is but one of many gifted writers who have explored the multiple identities of those migrants who know both the suffering and the sorrows of refugee life and the possibilities inherent in the struggle to transcend them.

Conclusion

What are some of the distinctive features of the contribution of cultural history to our understanding of modern war? The first and most salient achievement is to bring new and important insights into the history of extreme violence in armed conflict over the past century. The industrialization of war, the huge expansion in the power of the state, and the emergence of toxic ideologies laced with racial prejudice opened the door to an exponential growth of collective violence and a change in the norms surrounding it. From many points of view, political, social, and military historians have brought their learning to bear on accounting for war in what Eric Hobsbawm termed "the age of extremes."

Cultural historians have illuminated the darkness of these experiences. One example stands for many more. The early work of the great Australian cultural historian Inga Clendinnen focused on the culture of extreme violence in Mesoamerica before, during, and after the Spanish conquest. She then turned her attention to understanding the Shoah. As a result, she demolished the pretentions of those who would place the Shoah somehow outside of history. The tools of the cultural historian enabled her to rectify that error. Here is how she put it:

> Humankind saw the face of the Gorgon in the concentration camps, petrifying the human by its denial of the human, both in itself and in its prey . . . . If we are to see the Gorgon sufficiently steadily to destroy it, we cannot afford to be blinded by reverence or abashed into silence or deflected into a search for reassuring myths . . . neither reverence for those who suffer nor revulsion from those who inflict the suffering will help us overcome its power to paralyse, and to see it clearly.[64]

Clendinnen's book is a good example of two distinctive features of cultural history. The first is that cultural history is interdisciplinary at its core. Social anthropology provided Clendinnen with a conceptual framework and a way of handling the incendiary evidence of photographs and other

---

[63] www.nobelprize.org/prizes/literature/2021/summary.

[64] Clendinnen, *Reading the Holocaust*, p. 182.

artefacts of the Shoah. Instead of turning away from the horror in silence, she illuminated it.

Her insistence on the subject position of the historian and the need to be reflexive about it is a second central feature of the cultural history of war. Cultural historians do not do value-free social science. Our sense of self is embedded in our research, since extreme violence threatens the integrity of all of us. Being self-conscious about our personal stake in the story we tell about war and suffering is not a barrier to doing good history but a pathway toward the truth.

Clendinnen is but one of many cultural historians who have borrowed from neighboring disciplines in the social sciences and the humanities. As Peter Burke has noted, anthropology, literary history, and art history have inspired cultural historians to deepen their readings of practices, texts, and images.[65] As we have seen in our discussion of commemoration, testimony, and photography and painting, historians of war continue to benefit from avoiding what Burke terms the "frontier police" separating disciplines. Indeed, historians of war who venture into the complex domain of memory studies have returned the compliment, making major contributions to this multidisciplinary field.

Three of the pioneers of the field of the cultural history of war whose works we have cited crossed disciplinary frontiers. Paul Fussell was a professor of literature who combined personal experience of combat in the Second World War with a deep understanding of the language of irony. His 1975 publication *The Great War and Modern Memory* is a landmark. So is John Keegan's *The Face of Battle*, published the following year. It posed the question as to how soldiers withstand the stress of combat. Teaching at Sandhurst, he added to military history a cultural dimension by focusing on terror as an unavoidable feature of the face of battle. In 1979, the historian Eric Leed drew directly from the anthropologist Victor Turner's concept of liminality in his book *No Man's Land: Combat and Identity in World War I*.

The work of these and other scholars publishing in the 1970s established cultural history as an essential element in our understanding of the upheaval of the 1914–18 war. Many others have worked in later periods and in all parts of the globe. What these scholars share is a belief that cultural history, through its creative borrowing from other disciplines, helps us understand more fully the language, gestures, rituals, social articulations, and emotions of both soldiers and the societies that send them to war.

Furthermore, cultural history helps us see war as a layered phenomenon, a palimpsest in which more recent practices are written over but do not erase

---

[65] Peter Burke, *What is cultural history?* (Cambridge: Polity Press, 2008, 2nd ed.), p. 135.

earlier practices. We caution our readers against sharp distinctions between periods. The term "the interwar years," for example, makes little sense when set against the research on the ubiquity of armed conflict between 1918 and 1939. Cultural history shows that diplomats frequently fail to convert peace treaties into peace. We deal in tendencies, not clear divisions, even when we speak of the distinction between war and peace.

It would be foolish to ignore the overlaps between cultural histories of war and those produced by scholars in adjacent subdisciplines of history. All have a voice in the ongoing conversation about what war is and how it has changed over the past century. Focusing on the phenomenon of extreme violence, cultural historians of war have deepened our understanding not only on the changing face of armed conflict but also of the multiple ways men and women have survived the ravages of war with their humanity intact. That is no mean achievement.

Resources

Video files

1. Myra Hess playing at the National Gallery: www.youtube.com/watch?v=yaCg_nC2W5s
2. After effects of the bombing of Hiroshima: www.youtube.com/watch?v=n7fT6Mur6Gg
3. Yihiel Dinur testifying at Eichmann trial: www.youtube.com/watch?v=CBQo38mF-Ho&t=1202s
4. International Criminal Court for Rwanda, Decision in Nahimana trial: www.youtube.com/watch?v=JkVCfd1jybU
5. International Criminal Court for the former Yugoslavia, Decision in Mladic trial: www.youtube.com/watch?v=B2WVlBhjlW0

Audio files

1. Reading of letter to her son, from Vassily Grossman, *Life and Fate*, Anna's Letter: www.youtube.com/watch?v=q8xatKJGcK8
2. Benjamin Britten rehearses his "War Requiem": www.youtube.com/watch?v=LD8IxkQ96D4
3. Churchill's 'We shall never surrender' speech: www.youtube.com/watch?v=s_LncVnecLA&t=58s
4. Performance of Shostakovitch's Leningrad symphony: www.youtube.com/watch?v=kwqZRhPXElQ
5. Dimbleby report from Bergen-Belsen 1945: www.youtube.com/watch?v=VP9BLKZENbc

Bibliography

Abbenhuis, Maartje, Neill Atkinson, Kingsley Baird, and Gail Romano (eds.), *The myriad legacies of 1917: A year of war and revolution* (London: Palgrave Macmillan, 2018).

Akçam, Taner, *The Young Turks' crime against humanity: The Armenian genocide and ethnic cleansing in the Ottoman Empire* (Princeton, NJ: Princeton University Press, 2012).

Aksakal, Mustafa, "Holy war made in Germany?" Ottoman origins of the 1914 *jihad, War in History*, 18, 2 (April 2011), pp. 184–99.

Alcaide, Angel, The "brutalization thesis" (George L. Mosse) and its critics: A historiographical debate, *Pasado y memoria: Revista de historia contemporánea* (2016). https://doi.14198.PASADO 2016.15.01.

Altschuler, Mordechai, Jewish Holocaust commemorative activity in the USSR under Stalin, Yad Vashem, Shoah Resource Center. www.yadvashem.org /odot_pdf/Microsoft%20Word%20-%205422.pdf

Aly, Götz, *Hitler's beneficiaries: Plunder, racial war, and the Nazi welfare state* (New York: Metropolitan Books, 2007).

Ansky, S., *The enemy at his pleasure: A journey through the Jewish Pale of Settlement during World War I*, ed. and trans. by Joachim Neugroschel (New York: Metropolitan, 2002).

Ashworth, Tony, *Trench warfare, 1914–1918: The live and let live system* (New York: Holmes & Meyer, 1980).

Audoin-Rouzeau, Stéphane, and Annette Becker, *14–18: Retrouver la Grande Guerre* (Paris: Gallimard, 2003).

Balakian, Peter, *The black dog of fate: An American son uncovers his Armenian past* (New York: Broadway, 1997).

Baron, Nick, and Peter Gatrell (eds.), *Homelands: War, population and statehood in Eastern Europe and Russia, 1918–1924* (London: Anthem Press, 2004).

Barron, Stéphanie (ed.), *Exiles + emigrés: The flight of European artists from Hitler* (New York: Harry N. Abrams, 1997).

Bartov, Omer, *Anatomy of a genocide: The life and death of a town called Bugacz* (New York: Simon and Schuster, 2018).

Bartov, Omer, *Eastern Front 1941–45: German troops and the barbarization of warfare* (Basingstoke: Macmillan, 1985).

Bartov, Omer, Atina Grossmann, and Mary Nolan (eds.), *Crimes of war: Guilt and denial in the twentieth century* (New York: New Press, 2002).

Bartov, Omer, and Eric Weitz (eds.), *Shatterzones of empire: Coexistence and violence in the German, Habsburg, Russian and Ottoman borderlands* (Bloomington: Indiana University Press, 2013).

Bataković, Dušan T., Serbia's effort in the Great War: Testimonies, commemorations, interpretations, in *Cent ans après: La Mémoire de la première guerre mondiale*, ed. by Elli Lemonidou (Athens: Ecole Française d'Athènes, 2020), pp. 157–85.

Becker, Jean-Jacques, *Comment les Français sont entrées dans la Grande Guerre* (Paris: Presses de la Fondation Nationale des Sciences Politiques, 1977).

Best, Geoffrey, *Humanity in warfare: The modern history of the international law of armed conflicts* (London: Weidenfeld and Nicholson, 1980).

Beevor, Antony, and Lyuba Vinogradova, *A writer at war: Vasily Grossman with the Red Army, 1941–1945* (New York: Pantheon, 2006).

Beurier, Joëlle, *Photographier la Grande Guerre: France Allemagne: L'héroisme et la violence dans les magazines* (Rennes: Presses universitaires de Rennes, 2016).

Bloxham, Donald, *The great game of genocide: Imperialism, nationalism, and the destruction of the Ottoman Armenians* (Oxford: Oxford University Press, 2005).

Bohm-Duchen, Monica, *Art and the Second World War* (Farnham: Lund Humphries, 2013).

Bourke, Joanna, *Dismembering the male: Men's bodies, Britain and the Great War* (London: Reaktion, 1996).

Bourke, Joanna, *An intimate history of killing: Face-to-face killing in twentieth-century warfare* (London: Granta, 1999).

Browning, Christopher R., *Ordinary men: Reserve Police Battalion 101 and the final solution in Poland* (New York: Aaron Asher, 1992).

Burke, Peter, *What is cultural history?* (Cambridge: Polity Press, 2008, 2nd ed).

Cabanes, Bruno, *The Great War and the origins of humanitarianism 1918–1924* (Cambridge: Cambridge University Press, 2014).

Cabanes, Bruno, *La victoire endeuillée: La sortie de guerre des soldats français (1918–1920)* (Paris: Éditions du Seuil, 2004).

Carden-Coyne, Anna, *Reconstructing the body: Classicism, modernism and the First World War* (Oxford: Oxford University Press, 2009).

Clendinnen, Inga, *Reading the Holocaust* (Cambridge: Cambridge University Press, 2002).

Cohen, Deborah, *The war come home: Disabled veterans in Britain and Germany, 1914–1939* (Berkeley: University of California Press, 2001).

Damousi, Joy, *The labour of loss: Mourning, memory and wartime bereavement in Australia* (Cambridge: Cambridge University Press, 1999).

Das, Santanu, *India, empire and First World War culture: writings, images, and songs* (Cambridge: Cambridge University Press, 2018).

Das, Santanu (ed.), *Race, empire and First World War writing* (Cambridge: Cambridge University Press, 2011).

Diehl, James M., Change and continuity in the treatment of German *Kriegsopfer*, *Central European History*, 18, 2 (June 1985), pp. 170–87.

Dower, John W., *Cultures of war: Pearl Harbor, Hiroshima, 9–11, Iraq* (New York: W. W. Norton, 2010).

Dower, John W., *Embracing defeat: Japan in the wake of World War II* (New York: W. W. Norton, 1999).

Dower, John W., *Violent American century: War and terror since World War II* (Chicago: Haymarket, 2017).

Dower, John W., *War without mercy: Race and power in the Pacific War* (New York: Pantheon, 1986).

Eksteins, Modris, *Rites of spring: The Great War and the birth of the modern age* (Boston: Houghton Mifflin, 1989).

Engelstein, Laura, *Russia in flames: War, revolution, civil war, 1914–1921* (New York: Oxford University Press, 2017).

Farid, Samir M., Cohort nuptiality in England and Wales, *Population Studies*, 30, 1 (March 1976), pp. 137–51.

Farmer, Sarah, *Martyred village: Commemorating the 1944 massacre at Oradour-sur-Glane* (Berkeley: University of California Press, 1999).

Faron, Olivier, *Les enfants du deuil: Orphelins et pupilles de la nation de la premiere Guerre Mondiale (1914–1941)* (Paris: La Decouverte, 2001).

Fawaz, Leila-Tarazi, *A land of aching hearts: The Middle East in the Great War* (Cambridge, MA: Harvard University Press, 2014).

Fogarty, Richard, *Race and war in France: Colonial subjects in the French army, 1914–1918* (Baltimore, MD: Johns Hopkins University Press, 2008).

Fox, James, *British art and the First World War, 1914–1924* (Cambridge: Cambridge University Press, 2015).

Friedländer, Saul, *When memory comes*, trans. by Helen R. Lane (New York: Farrar, Straus, Giroux, 1979).

Fuller, John G., *Troop morale and popular culture in the British and Dominion armies 1914–1918* (Oxford: Clarendon, 1990).

Fussell, Paul, *The Great War and modern memory* (New York: Oxford University Press, 1975).

Fussell, Paul, *Wartime: Understanding and behavior in the Second World War* (New York: Oxford University Press, 1989).

Gammage, Bill, *The broken years: Australian soldiers in the Great War* (Canberra: Australian National University Press, 1974).

Gatrell, Peter, *The making of the modern refugee* (Oxford: Oxford University Press, 2013).

Gatrell, Peter, Refugees: What's wrong with history? *Journal of Refugee Studies*, 30, 2 (June 2017), pp. 170–89.

Gatrell, Peter, War, refugeedom, revolution: Understanding Russia's refugee crisis, 1914–1918, *Cahiers du monde russe*, 58, 1–2 (2017), pp. 123–46

Gatrell, Peter, *A whole empire walking: Refugees in Russia during World War I* (Bloomington: Indiana University Press, 1999).

Gerwarth, Robert, *Vanquished: Why the First World War failed to end, 1917–1923* (London: Allen Lane, 2016).

Gerwarth, Robert, and Donald Bloxham (eds.), *Political violence in twentieth-century Europe* (Cambridge: Cambridge University Press, 2011).

Gerwarth, Robert, and John Horne (eds.), *War in peace: Paramilitary violence in Europe after the Great War* (Oxford: Oxford University Press, 2013).

Gerwarth, Robert, and Erez Manela (eds.), *Empires at war, 1911–1923* (Oxford: Oxford University Press, 2014).

Geyer, Michael, and Adam Tooze (eds.), *The Cambridge history of the Second World War. Volume 3, Total war: Economy, society and culture* (Cambridge: Cambridge University Press, 2015).

Gildea, Robert, *Fighters in the shadows: A new history of the French Resistance* (Cambridge, MA: Harvard University Press, 2015).

Gildea, Robert, Olivier Wieviorka, and Anette Warring (eds.), *Surviving Hitler and Mussolini: Daily life in occupied Europe* (Oxford: Berg, 2006).

Gingeras, Ryan, *Sorrowful shores: Violence, ethnicity, and the end of the Ottoman Empire 1912–1923* (Oxford: Oxford University Press, 2009).

Goebel, Stefan, *The Great War and medieval memory: War, remembrance and medievalism in Britain and Germany, 1914–1940* (Cambridge: Cambridge University Press, 2007).

Grayzel, Susan R., *At home and under fire: Air raids and culture in Britain from the Great War to the Blitz* (New York: Cambridge University Press, 2012).

Gregory, Adrian, *The last great war: British society and the First World War* (Cambridge: Cambridge University Press, 2008).

Gregory, Adrian, *The silence of memory. Armistice Day, 1919–1946* (Oxford: Berg, 1994).

Gross, Jan T., *Fear: Anti-Semitism in Poland after Auschwitz* (New York: Random House, 2006).

Gross, Jan T., *Neighbors: The destruction of the Jewish community in Jedbawne, Poland* (Princeton, NJ: Princeton University Press, 2001).

Healy, Maureen, *Vienna and the fall of the Habsburg Empire: Total war and everyday life in World War I* (Cambridge: Cambridge University Press, 2004).

Higonnet, Margaret, and Patrice Higonnet, The double helix, in *Behind the lines: Gender and the two world wars*, ed. by Margaret Higonnet, Jane Jenson, Sonya Michel, and Margaret Collins Weitz (New Haven, CT: Yale University Press, 1987), pp. 31–50.

Higonnet, Margaret, Jane Jenson, Sonya Michel, and Margaret Collins Weitz (eds.), *Behind the lines: Gender and the two world wars* (New Haven, CT: Yale University Press, 1987).

Horne, John, Demobilizing the mind: France and the legacy of the Great War, 1919–1939, *French History and Civilization*, 2 (2009), pp. 101–19.

Horne, John, Demobilizing the mind, French civilization and culture. https://h-france.net/rude/wp-content/uploads/2017/08/vol2_Horne_Final_Version.pdf

Horne, John, and Alan Kramer, *German atrocities, 1914: A history of denial* (New Haven, CT: Yale University Press, 2001).

Houlihan, Patrick J., *Catholicism and the Great War: Religion and everyday life in Germany and Austria-Hungary, 1914–1922* (Cambridge: Cambridge University Press, 2015).

Huberband, Shimon, *Kiddush Hashem: Jewish religious and cultural life in Poland during the Shoah* (New York: Yeshiva University Press, 1987).

Hull, Isabel V., *Absolute destruction: Military culture and the practices of war in Imperial Germany* (Ithaca, NY: Cornell University Press, 2005).

Inglis, Ken, *Sacred places: War memorials in the Australian landscape* (Carlton, VIC: Melbourne University Press, 1998).

Inglis, Ken, Seumas Spark, and Jay Winter, *Dunera lives: A visual history* (Melbourne: Monash University Publications, 2018).

Joll, James, *1914: The unspoken assumptions* (London: London School of Economics, 1968).

Jones, Heather, *Violence against prisoners of war in the First World War: Britain, France and Germany, 1914–1920* (Cambridge, Cambridge University Press, 2011).

Kaldor, Mary, *New and old wars: Organized violence in a global era* (Cambridge: Polity Press, 1999).

Katznelson, Ira, *When affirmative action was white* (New York: W. W. Norton, 2005).

Keegan, John, *The face of battle: A study of Agincourt, Waterloo and the Somme* (London: Pimlico, 1976).

Kévorkian, Raymond, *Le Génocide des Arméniens* (Paris: Odile Jacob, 2006).

Kiernan, Ben, *Blood and soil: A world history of genocide and extermination from Sparta to Darfur* (New Haven, CT: Yale University Press, 2007).

Kicser, Hans-Lukas, Kerem Oktem, and Maurus Reimkowski (eds.), *World War I and the end of the Ottoman Empire: From the Balkan wars to the Turkish republic* (London: I. B. Tauris, 2015).

Kirschenbaum, Lisa, *The Legacy of the siege of Leningrad, 1941–1995: Myth, memories, and monuments* (Cambridge: Cambridge University Press, 2006),

Kramer, Alan, *Dynamic of destruction: Culture and mass killing in the First World War* (Oxford: Oxford University Press, 2007).

Kuzmarov, Jeremy, *The myth of the addicted army: Vietnam and the modern war on drugs* (Boston: University of Massachusetts Press, 2009).

Kwon, Heonik, *After the Korean War: An intimate history* (Cambridge: Cambridge University Press, 2020).

Kwon, Heonik, *Ghosts in Vietnam* (Cambridge: Cambridge University Press, 2004).

Kwon, Heonik, *Ghosts of war in Vietnam* (Cambridge: Cambridge University Press, 2008).

Lake, Marilyn, Henry Reynolds, Mark McKenna, and Joy Damousi, *What's wrong with Anzac?* (Sydney: New South Wales Press, 2010).

Leed, Eric J., *No man's land. Combat and identity in World War 1* (Cambridge: Cambridge University Press, 1979).

Leese, Peter, *Shell shock, traumatic neurosis and the British soldiers of the First World War* (New York: Palgrave/Macmillan, 2002).

Lemonidou, Elli (ed.), *Cent ans après: La Mémoire de la première guerre mondiale* (Athens: Ecole Française d'Athènes, 2020).

Leonhardt, Adrienne, Between two jailers: Women's experience during colonialism, war, and independence in Algeria, *Anthós*, 5, 1 (2013), pp. 43–54.

Lerner, Paul Frederick, *Hysterical men: War, psychiatry and the politics of trauma in Germany, 1890– 1930* (Ithaca, NY: Cornell University Press, 2003).

Liulevicius, Vejas Gabriel, *War land on the Eastern Front: Culture, national identity and German occupation in World War I* (Cambridge: Cambridge University Press, 2000).

Loez, André, *14–18. Les refus de la guerre. Une histoire des mutins* (Paris: Gallimard, 2010).

Lohr, Eric, *Nationalizing the Russian empire: The campaign against enemy aliens during World War I* (Cambridge, MA: Harvard University Press, 2003).

Lohr, Eric, The Russian army and the Jews: Mass deportation, hostages, and violence during World War I, *Russian Review*, 60, 3 (July 2001), pp. 404–19.

Manela, Erez, *The Wilsonian moment: Self-determination and the international origins of anticolonial nationalism* (New York: Oxford University Press, 2007).

Marrus, Michael, and Robert O. Paxton, *Vichy and the Jews* (New York: Basic Books, 1991).

McCartney, Helen B., *Citizen soldiers: The Liverpool Territorials in the First World War* (Cambridge: Cambridge University Press, 2006).

McNally, Richard J., Debunking myths about trauma and memory, *Canadian Journal of Psychiatry*, 1, 13 (November 2005), pp. 817–22.

Merridale, Catherine, *Ivan's war: Life and death in the Red Army, 1939–1945* (New York: Metropolitan Books, 2006).

Mitter, Rana, *China's good war: How World War II is shaping a new nationalism* (Cambridge, MA: Harvard University Press, 2020).

Mondini, Marco, *La guerra italiana: Partire, raccontare, tornare (1914–1918)* (Bologna: Il Mulino, 2014).

Mosse, George, *Fallen soldiers: Reshaping the memory of the world wars* (Oxford: Oxford University Press, 1990).

Murphy, Mahon, Carrier corps, in *1914–1918-online: International encyclopedia of the First World War*, ed. by Ute Daniel, Peter Gatrell, Oliver Janz, et al. (Berlin: Free University of Berlin, 2015). https://doi.org/10.15463/ie1418.10660

Nicholas, Lynn H., *The rape of Europa: The fate of Europe's treasures in the Third Reich and the Second World War* (New York: Knopf, 1994).

Oppenheim, Melanie, *The power of humanity: 100 years of Australian Red Cross* (Sydney: HarperCollins, 2014).

Overy, Richard, *Blood and ruins: The Great Imperial War, 1931–1945* (London: Allen Lane, 2021).

Palmieri, Daniel (ed.), *Le Comite international de la Croix-Rouge et la Grande Guerre* (Geneva: 14–18 Mission Centenaire, 2013).

Paxton, Robert O., *Collaboration and resistance: French literary life under the Nazi occupation* (New York: Five Ties, 2009).

Pedroncini, Guy, *1917: Les mutineries de l'armee francaise* (Paris: Julliard, 1968).

Pedersen, Susan, *The Guardians: The League of Nations and the crisis of Empire* (New York: Oxford University Press, 2017).

Petrone, Karen, *The Great War in Russian memory* (Bloomington: Indiana University Press, 2011).

Petropoulos, Jonathan, *Art as politics in the Third Reich* (Chapel Hill: University of North Carolina Press, 1996).

Petropoulos, Jonathan, *The Faustian bargain: The art world in Nazi Germany* (London: Penguin Press, 2000).

Pignot, Manon, *Allons enfants de la Patrie: Génération Grande Guerre* (Paris: Editions du Seuil, 2012).

Pignot, Manon, Children, in *The Cambridge History of the First World War*, vol. 3, ed. by Jay Winter (Cambridge: Cambridge University Press, 2014), p. 37.

Prost, Antoine, *Les anciens combattants et la société française, 1914–1939* (Paris: Presse de la Fondation Nationale des sciences politiques, 1977).

Prost, Antoine, The impact of war on French and German political cultures, *Historical Journal* (1994), pp. 128–54.

Rachamimov, Alon, *POWs and the Great War: Captivity on the Eastern Front* (Oxford: Berg, 2002).

Rakisits, Claude, Child soldiers in the east of the Democratic Republic of the Congo, *Refugee Survey Quarterly*, 27, 4 (2009), pp. 108–23.

Richard, Lionel, *L'art et la guerre: Les artistes confrontés à la seconde guerre mondiale* (Paris: Flammarion, 1995).

Robert, Jean-Louis, *Ouvriers, la patrie et la revolution: Paris, 1914–1919* (Paris: Les Belles Lettres, 1995).

Roberts, Mary Louise, *Civilization without sexes: Reconstructing gender in postwar France, 1917– 1927* (Chicago: University of Chicago Press, 1994).

Roberts, Mary Louise, *D-Day through French eyes: Normandy 1944* (Chicago: University of Chicago Press, 2014).

Rodogno, Davide, *Night on earth: A history of international humanitarianism in the Near East, 1918–1930* (Cambridge: Cambridge University Press, 2021).

Rose, Elihu, The anatomy of mutiny, *Armed Forces & Society*, 8, 4 (Summer 1982), pp. 561–74

Rother, Rainer (ed.), *Die UFA 1917–1945: Das deutsche Bildimperium* (Berlin: Deutsches Historisches Museum, Berlin, 1992).

Rozenblit, Marsha L., *Reconstructing a national identity: The Jews of Habsburg Austria during World War I* (New York: Oxford University Press, 2001).

Sands, Philippe, *East West Street: On the origins of "genocide" and "crimes against humanity"* (New York: Alfred A. Knopf, 2016).

Sands, Philippe, *The Ratline Love, lies and justice on the trail of a Nazi fugitive* (London: Weidenfeld and Nicolson, 2020).

Scates, Bruce, *A place to remember: A history of the Shrine of Remembrance* (Cambridge: Cambridge University Press, 2009).

Scates, Bruce, Rebecca Wheatley, and Laura James, *World War One: A history in 100 stories* (Melbourne: Penguin, 2015).

Schivelbusch, Wolfgang, *The culture of defeat: On national trauma, mourning and recovery* (New York: Metropolitan Books, 2003).

Sherman, Daniel J., *The construction of memory in interwar France* (Chicago: University of Chicago Press, 1999).

Siebrecht, Claudia, *The aesthetics of loss. German women's art of the First World War* (Oxford: Oxford University Press, 2013).

Silver, Kenneth E., *Esprit de corps: The art of the Parisian avant-garde and the First World War, 1914–25* (Princeton, NJ: Princeton University Press, 1989).

Sivan, Emmanuel, *Radical Islam: Medieval theology and modern politics* (New Haven, CT: Yale University Press, 1985).

Sivan, Emmanuel, Yizkor books and commemoration in Israel in 1948, in *War and remembrance in the twentieth century*, ed. by Jay Winter and Emmanuel Sivan (Cambridge: Cambridge University Press, 1999), pp. 168–95.

Smith, Leonard V., *Between mutiny and obedience: The case of the French Fifth Infantry Division in World War I* (Princeton, NJ: Princeton University Press, 1994).

Smith, Leonard V., *Sovereignty at the Paris Peace Conference of 1919* (Oxford: Oxford University Press, 2018).

Snyder, Timothy, *Black earth: The Holocaust as history and warning* (New York: Tim Duggan Books, 2015).

Snyder, Timothy, *Bloodlands: Between Hitler and Stalin* (New York: Basic Books, 2010).

Stansky, Peter, and William Abrahams, *London's burning: Life, death, and art in the Second World War* (Stanford, CA: Stanford University Press, 1994).

Stites, Richard, and Ariel Roshwald (eds.), *European culture in the Great War: The arts, entertainment and propaganda, 1914–1918* (Cambridge: Cambridge University Press, 1999).

Suny, Ronald Grigor, *"They can live in the desert but nowhere else": A history of the Armenian genocide* (Princeton, NJ: Princeton University Press, 2015).

Tetsuya, Fujiwara, Disabled war veterans during the Allied occupation of Japan, trans. by Ruselle Meade, *SOAS Occasional Translations in Japanese Studies* (3) 2012. www.soas.ac.uk/jrc/translations/file76257.pdf

Thomson, Alistair, *Anzac memories: Living with the legend* (Clayton: Monash University Press, 2013).

Tippett, Maria, *Art at the service of war: Canada, art and the Great War* (Toronto: University of Toronto Press, 1984).

Todman, Dan, *The First World War: Myth and memory* (London: Hambledon, 2005).

Vance, Jonathan, *Death so noble: Memory, meaning and the First World War* (Vancouver: University of British Columbia Press, 1997).

Vance, Jonathan, *The Great War: From memory to history* (Waterloo: Wilfrid Laurier University Press, 2015).

Verhey, Jeffrey, *The spirit of 1914: Militarism, myth and mobilization in Germany* (Cambridge: Cambridge University Press, 2000).

Vidal-Naquet, Clementine, *Couples dans la Grande Guerre: Le tragique et l'ordinaire du lien conjugal* (Paris: Les Belles Lettres, 2014).

Vidal-Naquet, Clementine, *La Grande Guerre des Francais a travers les archives de la Grande Collecte* (Paris: Mission du centenaire de la Premiere Guerre Mondiale, 2018).

Virgili, Fabrice, *La France "virile": Des femmes tondues à la Libération* (Paris: Payot, 2000).

Vondung, Klaus (ed.), *Kriegserlebnis: Der Erste Weltkrieg in der literarischen Gestaltung und Symbolischen Deutung der Nationen* (Gottingen: Vandenhoeck and Ruprecht, 1980).

Watenpaugh, Keith David, *Bread from stones: The Middle East and the making of modern humanitarianism* (Oakland: University of California Press, 2015).

Watenpaugh, Keith David, The League of Nations' rescue of Armenian genocide survivors and the making of modern modern humanitarianism, 1920–1927, *American Historical Review*, 115, 5 (December 2010), pp. 1315–39.

Watkins, Glenn, *Proof through the night: Music and the Great War* (Berkeley: University of California Press, 2003).

Watson, Alexander, *Enduring the Great War: Combat, morale and collapse in the German and British armies, 1914–1918* (Cambridge: Cambridge University Press, 2008).

Wieviorka, Annette, *The era of the witness*, trans. by Jared Stark (Ithaca, NY: Cornell University Press, 2006).

Wilcox, Vanda, *Morale and the Italian army during the First World War* (Cambridge: Cambridge University Press, 2016).

Wilson, Edmond, *Patriotic gore: Studies in the literature of the American Civil War* (New York: W. W. Norton, 1962).

Winter, Jay (ed.), *The Cambridge history of the First World War* (Cambridge: Cambridge University Press, 2014).

Winter, Jay, *The Day the Great War ended, 24 July 1923: The civilianization of war* (Oxford: Oxford University Press, 2022).

Winter, Jay, *The Great War and the British people* (London: Macmillan, 1985).

Winter, Jay, The Great War and Jewish memory, *Yearbook for European Jewish Literature Studies*, 1 (2014), pp. 13–41.

Winter, Jay, *Remembering war: The Great War between history and memory* (New Haven, CT: Yale University Press, 2007).

Winter, Jay, War and anxiety in 1917, in *The myriad legacies of 1917: A year of war and revolution*, ed. by Maartje Abbenhuis, Neill Atkinson, Kingsley Baird, and Gail Romano (London: Palgrave Macmillan, 2018), pp. 13–33.

Winter, Jay, *War beyond words: Languages of remembrance from the Great War to the present* (Cambridge: Cambridge University Press, 2017).

Winter, Jay, and Antoine Prost, *René Cassin and human rights: From the Great War to the Universal Declaration* (Cambridge: Cambridge University Press, 2012).

Winter, Jay, and Jean-Louis Robert (eds.), *Capital cities at war: Paris, London, Berlin, 1914–1919. A cultural history* (Cambridge: Cambridge University Press, 2008).

Winter, Jay, and Emmanuel Sivan (eds.), *War and remembrance in the twentieth century* (Cambridge: Cambridge University Press, 1999).

Xu, Guoqi, *Strangers on the Western Front: Chinese workers in the Great War* (Cambridge, MA: Harvard University Press, 2011).

Ziemann, Benjamin, *Contested commemorations: Republican war veterans and Weimar political culture* (Cambridge: Cambridge University Press, 2013).

Ziemann, Benjamin, *Front und Heimat: Landliche Kriegserfahrunger im sudlichen Bayern 1914–1923* (Essen: Klartest, 1997).

Ziemann, Benjamin, *Violence and the German soldier in the Great War: Killing, dying, surviving*, translated by Andrew Evans (London: Bloomsbury Academic, 2017).

Ziino, Bart, *A distant grief: Australians, war graves, and the Great War* (Perth: University of Western Australia Press, 2007).

Acknowledgments

This book represents the fruits of conversations over many years. They started with my first teacher, Fritz Stern, at Columbia University in 1966. They have continued with students at the Hebrew University of Jerusalem in the 1970s, then at Cambridge, and finally at Yale. In particular, these brief essays on inexhaustible topics remind me of the pleasures of the supervision system at Cambridge, where my students were set a weekly assignment to write a ten-page essay on a huge topic backed up by formidable reading lists. In this Element, I have tried to do a bit of the same. I have aimed at synthesis and argument above all, and I hope I have disclosed to readers some of the richness of the now abundant and frequently moving literature on the cultural history of war.

My colleagues in the Research Centre of the Historial de la Grande Guerre at Péronne enabled me to frame these questions and configure answers as part of a collective. Participation in this project changed my life and enriched it in ways that I hope are evident to the reader.

There are so many colleagues with whom I have explored this subject that I cannot pretend to list all of them who gave me ideas, suggested sources, contested my arguments, and tolerated my enthusiasms. To John Horne and Antoine Prost, friends of forty years, I owe more than I can say.

Harvey Mendelsohn, Vanda Wilcox, and Kolleen Guy took the time to read the manuscript and smooth it out. Any errors that remain in this book are mine and mine alone.

Cambridge Elements $\equiv$

Modern Wars

General Editor

Robert Gerwarth

University College Dublin

Robert Gerwarth is Professor of Modern History at University College Dublin and Director of UCD's Centre for War Studies. He has published widely on the history of political violence in twentieth-century Europe, including an award-winning history of the aftermath of the Great War, *The Vanquished*, and a critically acclaimed biography of Reinhard Heydrich, the chief organizer of the Holocaust. He is also the general editor of Oxford University Press's Greater War series, and, with Jay Winter, general editor of Cambridge University Press's Studies in the Social and Cultural History of Modern Warfare series.

Editorial Board

Heather Jones, *University College London*

Rana Mitter, *University of Oxford*

Michelle Moyd, *Indiana University, Bloomington*

Martin Thomas, *University of Exeter*

About the Series

Focusing on the flourishing field of war studies (broadly defined to include social, cultural and political perspectives), Elements in Modern Wars examine the forms, manifestations, and legacies of violence in global contexts from the mid-nineteenth century to the present day.

Cambridge Elements ☰

Modern Wars

Elements in the Series

The Cultural History of War in the Twentieth Century and After
Jay Winter

A full series listing is available at: www.cambridge.org/EMOW

Printed in the United States
by Baker & Taylor Publisher Services